Oh, How We Danced!

Elizabeth Casciani was born in Durham and raised in Fife. After a stay in Glasgow she moved to Edinburgh where she now lives. Her first article appeared in the Edinburgh *Evening Dispatch* when she was still at school. Since then, while working as a teacher and in the field of advertising, she has been widely published as a freelance writer, both of fiction and non-fiction. She has also been a frequent writer and broadcaster on BBC and commercial radio, and regularly gives talks on story and article writing to clubs and schools. Currently she is a freelance researcher. Widowed in 1993, she has four children and two grand-children.

THE HISTORY OF BALLROOM DANCING IN SCOTLAND

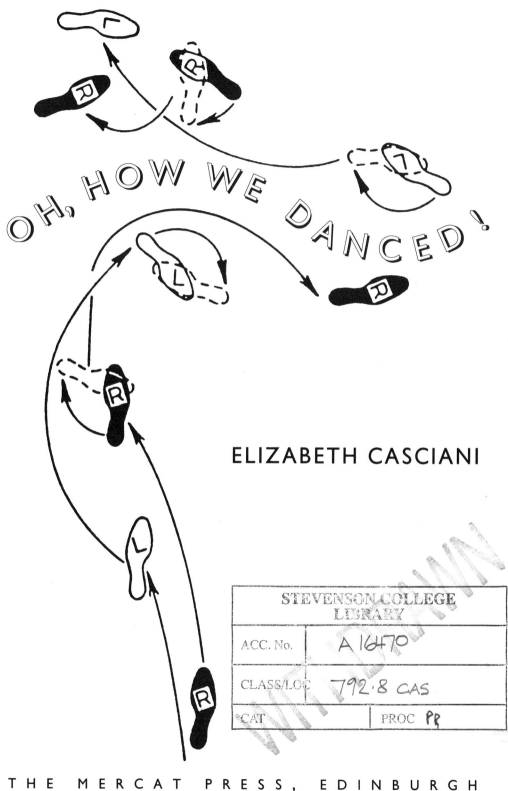

OH, HOW WE DANCED!

ELIZABETH CASCIANI

THE MERCAT PRESS, EDINBURGH

First published in 1994 by Mercat Press
James Thin, 53 South Bridge, Edinburgh EH1 1YS

ISBN 1873644299

Typeset by Servis Filmsetting Ltd., Manchester
Printed in Great Britain by
The Cromwell Press, Melksham

Contents

List of Illustrations   vi

Preface   viii

1   Aristocratic Assemblies: the Eighteenth Century   1

2   Popular Assemblies: the Nineteenth Century   18

3   Growth of the Dancing Schools: 1900 to 1910   30

4   Flappers and Fox Trots: 1910 to 1920   40

5   Rise of the Big Palais Ballrooms: 1920 to 1930   48

6   Big Bands and Scandals: 1930 to 1940   66

7   Crooners and Championships: 1940 to 1950   95

8   From Couples to Individuals: 1950 to the Present   108

Epilogue: the End of an Era?   127

Notes to the text   131

Appendix 1   135

Appendix 2   136

Index   137

Illustrations

The first Assembly Rooms in Edinburgh	2
Susanna, Duchess of Eglinton	5
A directress' badge of office	6
Minuet at the Assembly	11
The new Assembly Rooms in Edinburgh	16
The Assembly Rooms in Glasgow	17
A fast Waltz	20
A dance programme	23
The Warren family in 1908	32
The Marine Gardens, Portobello	36
Mr and Mrs J Warren	41
Bunny Hug bumpers	42
The Albert	46
Robert Sielle and Annette Mills	51
Dancers at the Locarno	53
A ballroom on Sunday	56
The manager and owner of the Marine Gardens	57
The staff of the Marine Gardens	59
Visiting celebrities at the Marine Gardens	60
Tim Wright's band at the Plaza	61
Columbia prizes	63
John Warren and Dorothy Dawn	69
A novelty race	70
Louis Freeman	73
The band on board the Dilwara	74
Harry Smead and his Boys	75
Matt Lind of the Colorado Band	77
The doormen at the Edinburgh Plaza	79
Joe Loss	81
Finals of the Scottish Dancing Championship	86
Alex Warren in 1931	87
Committee of the Scottish Dance Teachers' Alliance	88
The Coronation Dance Team	89
George Dundas and Bertha Wilson	90
The Excelsior Ballroom	91
Andy Lothian's band	92

Prominent figures in the Edinburgh dance scene	96
Billy MacGregor	98
A group of dancers at Paulena's	100
Bert Valentine and band	105
Televised lessons for children	109
A group of Championship judges in 1955	110
A youthful Farquhar MacRae	111
Paul Collins with his formation dance team	112
East of Scotland Old Time Dancing Championship	113
Tim Wright and his band	114
Valerie Anne Brown dancing with her grandfather	117
Valerie Anne Brown twisting the Madison	118
Bob Barty leading the dancers in Dundee	120
Warren Brown and Aileen Turner	122
Warren Brown jnr. and Rebecca Hannant	123
Bill and Bobby Irvine	124
Donny Burns and Gaynor Fairweather	125

Preface

I have always loved dancing, but lack of opportunity to practise has left me close to the category of the lady in Gilbert and Sullivan who 'doesn't think she dances but would rather like to try'. This book is the follow-up to an article I wrote for the *Scots Magazine* in 1980 on the demise of the Edinburgh Plaza. I discovered that, while there were many books on how to dance, and about famous dances and dancers, there seemed to be none about the thousands of people who danced – people like myself who enjoyed dancing.

I was fortunate to be allowed to visit the Plaza three weeks before it was razed to the ground to make way for a supermarket. We climbed dark and dusty stairs to the main ballroom and, while I waited in the silence, my guide threw on the lights. We were standing on a floor that gleamed like yellow silk, and overhead a dusty mirrored ball showered us with snowflakes of light. I felt suddenly as if, at any moment, the dancers would step from behind the pillars and bring the ballroom to life. I was hooked from that moment. I knew I had to write their story.

It seemed logical to begin at the beginning with the first ballroom I could find in Scotland, which took me back to 1710. I never dreamed that the quest for information would take so long and involve so many people. It has left me with an abiding interest in this part of our social history. Inevitably, the story is incomplete, because everybody has a story to tell. I still hope to hear from anyone who would like to share memories with me, and I have a particular interest in copies of magazines like the *Scottish Dancing Journal* or any other dancing ephemera.

Dancing, I discovered, is a healthy pursuit, and I have been privileged to meet many people able to dance well into their eighties. Farquhar MacRae is a shining example who, in his ninetieth year, still dances three times a week. It is impossible to name individually the hundreds of dancers who have given generously of their time to talk to me. I must use the following names as examples and ask the others also to accept my most grateful thanks.

Mr and Mrs Bob Barty; Mr and Mrs John Banks; Mr J Bennett; Mr Bill Braidie; Mr and Mrs Warren Brown; Mr A Bryce; Mr Donny Burns and Gaynor Fairweather; Mr Andrew Bathgate; Mr Gerry Davis; Lord Bernard Delfont; Mrs Bertha Dundas; Mr Maurice Fleming; Mr Clifford Hanley; Mrs Marjorie Harkins; Mr H Hawthorn; Mrs Sylvia Hume; Mr Bill Irvine; Mrs Valerie Horn; Mr D McBain; Mr John McCormack; Mr Billy MacGregor; Ms Gwen McIlroy; Mr J Mackenzie; Mr P McLauchlan (SABDA); Mr F MacRae; Mr Barrie Marshall; Mr Bill Martin (Musician's Union); Mr T Morton; Mr J Reavely; Mr John Rundle; Mr Ron Self; Mr A Sharp; Mr K Smith; Mr Bert Valentine; Mr J Wishart.

Thanks also to the late: Mr Louis Freeman; Mr T Gauld; Miss D Glendinning; Mrs J Herbertson; Ms E Linton; Mr A Lothian; Mr J Loss; Mrs B McCall; Mr J McFarlane; Mrs E Middleton; Mrs P Moffat; Mr C Robbie; Mr J Smith; Mr A Warren: who gave generous help in the last years of their lives.

Finally, grateful thanks to Mr Douglas Russell, my computer guru, without whose help this book would never have been completed.

CHAPTER ONE

Aristocratic Assemblies

୶ଵ ଵ୶

The Eighteenth Century

The story of dance in Scotland has a long and ancient history but ballroom dancing by definition implies the existence of a ballroom and is relatively recent.

A *Ball* was defined as early as 1632 as 'a social assembly for the purpose of dancing'[1] and those who attended the Ball were 'often people belonging to the same or a connected establishment, society, profession etc, with an organised programme'.[2] An *Assembly* was 'a stated and general meeting of the polite persons of both sexes for the sake of conversation, gallantry, news and play.'[3] It was also described as 'a gathering of persons for purposes of social entertainment'.[4]

There were other kinds of entertainment. A *Masquerade* or *Masked Ball* was an occasion for pageantry and revelry which earned it an unsavoury reputation. A *Ridotto* was a musical evening in which the audience was entertained by singers in the first half of the evening followed by a second half when everyone danced. A *Rout* was a large evening party or reception held in a private house.

Assemblies were first established in Scotland during the eighteenth century, although ballroom dancing was then restricted to those with 'at least a just title to gentility'.[5] Troubled years of religious and political unrest had left Scotland poverty-stricken and, at the beginning of the eighteenth century, the Presbyterian Church frowned upon dancing in public as frivolous. John Knox had earlier laid down the law to Mary Queen of Scots and this influenced the attitude of the Church. In 1562 he had pronounced:

> Dancing, Madam, albeit in Scripture I find no praise of it, and in profane writings, that it is termed the gesture rather of them that are mad and in frenzy than of sober men: yet I do not utterly condemn it, provided two vices be avoided: the former that the principal vocation of those who use that exercise be not neglected for the pleasure of dancing, and secondly, that they dance not, as the Philistines their fathers, for the pleasure that they take in the displeasure of God's people.[6]

The first Assembly Rooms in Edinburgh in the West Bow, a narrow street that once wound from the Grassmarket to Castlehill. The buildings were demolished about 1836 when Victoria Street and Terrace were constructed

So, Scots could dance provided that they did not neglect their work or dance simply to spite the minister!

In any case, in the Scottish countryside few had time or money to spend on the luxuries and trappings of assemblies. One parish minister recorded:

> Instead of meeting at large assemblies . . . each family collects and spends time in eating, drinking and conversation. People even celebrate their marriages without company of dancing. Some of the sectaries punish attendance on penny weddings and public dancing with reproof from the pulpit in presence of the congregation.[7]

(At penny weddings the guests paid for their food, drink and entertainment because neither the couple nor their parents could afford the expense. The proceeds were supposed to go to the bride and groom.)

However, in the early eighteenth century, although the roads were still so bad that few people travelled far, those who did travel brought news of gaieties at the French Court and of the famous new Assembly at Bath presided over by Beau Nash. Some felt that the capital city of Edinburgh should be like other places and allow greater freedom in the organisation of entertainment. In what was a direct challenge to the old ways, in 1705, John, 3rd Earl of Selkirk, formed the fashionable 'Horn Order' in Edinburgh, adopting a horn spoon as a badge. A small gathering of ladies and gentlemen braved the wrath of the Scottish Church and enjoyed dancing the Minuet. Masquerades were also held and there were accusations of promiscuity and scandal.

Five years later, in 1710, the first regular Assembly was held in the city in a building in the West Bow on a site now occupied by St John's Free Church.[8] Feelings ran high in the city, especially in the area of the West Bow, where the inhabitants were particularly devoted to the cause of the Covenant. It was reported that on one occasion an infuriated mob of zealots assaulted the company and attacked the door of the assembly room, perforating it with red-hot spits.[9]

This first assembly room was not particularly suited to the purpose but at least it established a place to dance, as we can see from this description by a nine-teenth century writer:

Ascending by a narrow spiral stair we come to the second floor now occupied by a dealer in wool but presenting such appearances as to leave no doubt that it once con-sisted of a single lofty wainscotted room with a carved oak ceiling. Here did the fair ladies whom Allan Ramsay and William Hamilton celebrate meet for the recreation of dancing with their toupeed and deep-skirted beaux.[10]

Ministers preached against the assembly from their pulpits but, despite all opposition, the West Bow Assembly flourished for the next ten years. Alexander Ballantyne, who lived there at the time, described the fashionables of the city flocking down the street in their magnificent dresses and how the ladies held up their trains as they ascended to the ballroom. The whole Bow was packed full of sedan chairs and carriages. Most of the women wore pattens on their feet to protect themselves from the filth underfoot.

Robert Chambers describes the dress at this time. It included calashes (hoods); bongraces (bonnets); capuchins (short cloaks); negligees (gowns using about 10 yards of material); stomachers (a triangular piece of silk worn point down over the stomach); stays (corsets worn long enough to touch the chair at front and rear when seated); petticoats (often more splendid than the gown); hoops (pocket hoops like panniers for the morning, bell hoops for the afternoon and full hoops for the evening. The evening hoops were 'so monstrous that people saw one half of it enter the room before the wearer'); embroidered garters; a lappet (Brussels lace streamers hanging down the back of the head from the crown); plaids (shawls to cover heads and faces when out of doors); knots of ribbons for adornment and ear-rings, necklaces, bracelets and pong-pongs (a jewel fixed to a wire with a long pin at the end worn at the front of the cap so that it shook when the wearer moved); and thick silk or linen stockings slashed with contrasting colour or decorated with gold or silver clocks. These were often scarlet silk and worn by men and women.

Shoes were high-heeled set off with fine lace or sewn work and sharply pointed at the front.

3

Finally, there were the fans, which were large, with sticks of curiously carved wood or painted leather from Italy or Holland.

The popularity of the assemblies made it necessary to move to larger premises, a move which aroused more opposition. The dancers found a champion in Allan Ramsay who, in June 1723, published a poem called *The Fair Assembly* extolling the effects of dancing on health and deportment. His preface, addressed to 'The Right Honourable Ladies', began:

> How much is our whole nation indebted to your Ladyships for your reasonable and laudable undertaking to introduce politeness among us, by a cheerful entertainment, which is highly for the advantage of both body and mind, in all that is becoming in the brave and beautiful . . . It is amazing to imagine that any are so destitute of good sense and manners as to drop the least unfavourable sentiment against the Fair Assembly.[11]

The new Assembly opened in 1723 in Patrick Steil's Close (now the Old Assembly Close on the south side of the High Street between St Giles and the Tron Kirk). In Chambers' *Domestic Annals of Scotland* it was described prosaically as 'an arrangement for a weekly meeting of the younger people of both sexes for the purpose of dancing'.[12]

Miss Anne Stuart, the niece of the Earl of Moray, wrote from Donibristle to a friend in Muirton,

> They have got an assembley at Edinburgh where every Thursday they meet and dance from four o'clock to eleven at night; it is half a crown the ticket and whatever tea, coffee, chocalate [sic], biscuit etc. they call for, they must pay as the managers direct. The ministers are preaching against it and say it will be another horn order.[13]

In the ten years from 1723 to 1733, there were 255 meetings – an average of 25 a year. From the outset, these assemblies were conducted in an orderly manner. Only the cream of society was admitted, their sedan chairs arriving at 4 pm and departing punctually at 11 pm.

Edward Burt, who visited Edinburgh in 1724, attended the assembly and wrote to a friend, 'I do not indeed remember there was much disturbance at the institution of the ball or assembly, because that meeting is chiefly composed of people of distinction'.[14]

There was one complaint in an anonymous pamphlet that young serving girls could not be persuaded to go to bed early, preferring to stand in the High Street to watch the departure of the rich and beautiful dancers; and that the time spent in church was considerably less than the seven hours of the Assembly.

One who always excited attention was Susanna Kennedy, Duchess of Eglinton, who came with her seven daughters in sedan chairs from their home in the Canongate. The elegant Susanna was six feet tall and famed for her complexion of bewitching loveliness which she never painted with make-up, although she

The lovely Susanna, Duchess of Eglinton
(*By courtesy of the National Portrait Gallery, Edinburgh*)

washed her face periodically with sow's milk. She was described as the most beautiful woman at a Hunter's Ball in Holyrood House in 1732 when she wore a large hoop and a suit of gold-trimmed black velvet.

About 1736 the Assembly had to move again when the tenancy came to an end. On 25 May 1736 it opened in new premises between Bell's Wynd and Stevenlaw's Close (now 142 High Street).

'The Right Honourable Company of Hunters' now held an annual Ball in the Palace of Holyrood House. On 21 December, 1736, it was reported, 'There were two rooms for dancing, and two for tea, illuminated with many hundreds of wax candles. In the Grand Hall [the Gallery?] a table was covered with three hundred dishes *en ambigu*, at which sate a hundred and fifty ladies at a time . . . illuminated with four hundred wax candles.'[15]

By this time there were dancing assemblies in some of the other principal towns in Scotland, notably Dundee and Aberdeen. On 27 January 1737 the young gentlemen-burghers of Aberdeen gave a grand ball to the ladies, the most splendid and numerous ever seen there, which, it was claimed, was all conducted without the least confusion or disorder.

The organisation of assemblies was a serious and formal affair. An Assembly Committee appointed directresses to be in charge of each function. Money raised went to charity. The Royal Infirmary and the Poorhouse were early beneficiaries. Amongst the ladies who held office were the Countess of Panmure, Lady Newhall, Lady North Berwick, Lady Drummelier and Lady Ormiston. The directresses wore distinctive badges of office, one of which has survived and can be seen at the National Museum of Antiquities in Edinburgh.

The directresses had the power to refuse entry to anyone considered unsuitable although, according to Edward Burt, they did not exclude 'strangers of good appearance'.[16] No doubt his own acceptance on his visit from London was a source of some satisfaction.

The considerable powers of the directresses extended to the selection of the dancers and the order in which they were called to dance. They even made regulations about the clothes dancers wore. Newspapers in 1728 reported that 'All ladies and gentlemen were to come to the Assembly twice a year dressed entirely in the manufactures of the country and at all times thereafter no linen or lace was to be worn in this assembly but what it shall be made in Great Britain'.[17] (Surely, the first recorded 'Buy British' campaign!)

In 1740 a severe winter caused much suffering amongst the poor in Edinburgh and a special assembly was arranged for 7 February to raise funds. Tickets cost ten shillings and sixpence and all proceeds were to be distributed instantly to the needy.

It was recorded that card and dancing assemblies were very fashionable in

The badge worn by the Directress of an Assembly. (© *The Trustees of the National Museums of Scotland 1994*)

Glasgow too from the middle to the close of the century. Glasgow was a small town at the beginning of the eighteenth century with none of the sophistication of Edinburgh. In his autobiography, Dr Alexander Carlyle wrote that at this time 'There were only a few families of ancient citizens pretending to be gentlemen. The rest were shopkeepers and mechanics and successful pedlars . . . their manner of life was coarse and vulgar.'[18]

It was not until 1758, when the population of Glasgow had risen to about thirty-five thousand, that a regular coach drawn by four horses covered the forty-two miles to Edinburgh in twelve hours, the passengers stopping to dine on the way. As Glasgow grew and communication improved, there was an increased interest in assemblies.

The first proper assembly hall in Glasgow was situated at the west end of the Tontine Buildings in the Trongate. The new hall was erected by a subscription of the tobacco lords (the merchant princes of Glasgow who had made fortunes by trading in tobacco from Virginia in America) and neighbouring country gentry. It was sold to the Tontine Society who built a new assembly room in 1783 which was in use until 1796.

> Dancing assemblies attracted the whole rank and fashion from the West; daughters and sons of ancient country families came by coach or on horseback from their country mansions to balls that began at 5 o'clock and lasted till 11 pm, mingling with a touch of condescension with the new families of prosperous merchants.[19]

Later, when assemblies began at 8 pm, the regulations requested that gentlemen 'do not appear in their boots'and that they 'leave their sticks at the bar'.

Ladies in fashion wore hoops and silks, powdered their hair and carried long green fans. The men wore bright coloured coats and scarlet waistcoats and they also had powdered hair.

Senex wrote in the *Glasgow Herald* in 1856:

> I remember being at an assembly in the Tontine Room when George, Duke of Argyll, then a fine looking young man, led down the Country Dance with the beautiful Nancy Bogle, at that time the reigning toast of the city. They were the handsomest couple in the room. When a nobleman was present at our assemblies, he took the head of the Country Dance from courtesy, the drawing for place being dispensed with in his favour; he also selected the figure of the dance.[20]

The dancing season lasted from mid-November to mid-April with an average of 24 dances during the season. By 1780 the dancing assemblies had to resort to a General Subscription since the money taken at the door did not cover expenses. Gentlemen were charged one guinea for the season and ladies were charged nothing. The Tobacco Lords made it difficult for wives and daughters of shopkeepers in the city to mix with the 'aristocracy' in the course of the dances.

New assembly rooms were built to a design by Robert and James Adam who both died before work began on the north side of Ingram Street in 1796. It boasted a grand frontage with four Ionic Columns and the interior was equally grand.

In Glasgow, dancers appeared to favour sets of twelve.

> Chairs were set with their backs to the dancers along the north wall leaving a space behind for the spectators. Three violins, a violincello and a flute generally supplied the music and the most popular dances were Cotillons and sprightly Country Dances. Slow-going Minuets were never much in vogue here. The most popular tunes at the time were 'Brose and Butter', 'Flowers of Edinburgh' and 'Monymusk'.[21]

In Scotland at this period, dancing music was generally accompanied by bagpipes or violin. In 1746, following the rebellion of 1745, the Act of Proscription was passed, aimed at eliminating Highland culture by banning the wearing of kilts and the playing of bagpipes. This opened the way for the violin to become the national instrument of Scotland.

Noted musicians of the time were Robert Bremner, who published his *Collection of Reels and Country Dances* in 1761; John Riddell, composer and publisher of Reels and Strathspeys including the popular 'The Merry Lads of Ayr'; Francis Peacock, who published a book with the weighty title, *Sketches relative to the History and Theory, but more especially to the Practice of Dancing, as a necessary accomplishment to the Youth of both Sexes*; Daniel Dow, a composer of Strathspeys and Reels including the highly popular 'Monymusk', 'The Brig o' Perth' and 'The Duchess of Gordon'; and James Scott Skinner from Deeside, self-dubbed 'The Strathspey King' and arguably Scotland's greatest fiddle composer. Most famous of all was Neil Gow who founded a dynasty of violinists and himself led the music at many of the assemblies.[22]

Early assemblies were often cold and draughty and, to make matters worse, smoke from the sedan bearers' torches blew in through the open doors so that by mid-evening, chaperones and dancers risked pneumonia or asphyxiation.

In Edinburgh, partners were usually selected at a private party before the ball. The story goes that ladies dropped their fans into a gentleman's cocked hat and the gentlemen were invited to choose a fan.[23] As these couples would remain partners for the whole year it is at least possible that the gentlemen may have been primed by the ladies of their choice as to the fan they selected. Failing this, their only hope of meeting the partner they desired was to beg the directress to include them in the same set. Gentlemen could make a direct appeal but young ladies had to depend on the negotiating powers of their chaperones.

> The tickets were then bought by the gentleman, who sometimes had one or two oranges stowed away in his coat pocket for the refreshment of his lady, who sucked them during pauses in conversation and intervals in the dance – a succulent process which she varied by presenting to her nose delicate pinches of snuff which she extracted from the dainty snuff-box hanging by her side. Some of the gentlemen also carried muffs to conceal a mutton pie or a slice of salmon in case they felt hungry during the evening.[24]

The customary price for the ticket was two shillings and sixpence. The modest expenses of tea and coffee which were consumed in the card room were extra.

Tickets were sold in Edinburgh by the bookseller, Gavin Hamilton. It was he who, at the end of the lease of the building in 1746, came to the rescue and set up a new assembly. He did this in a business-like manner, involving other city businessmen as directors in a kind of management takeover. With James Stirling he took over the rent of the building at his own risk for £55 a year. From then on an Assembly Minute Book kept a clear record of events. New gold badges were struck for the directresses bearing, on one side, a pelican feeding her young, with the motto 'Charity', and on the other side, figures of a woman and child with the motto 'Edinburgh'.

Music was supplied by an orchestra of four fiddles, one bassoon and two hautboys playing Minuets to tunes such as 'Lady Murray of Clermont' and 'Mrs Campbell of Shawfield'. Fergusson claimed that the music was the weak point at these balls and it was by no means equal to the dancing. One fiddler describing a fellow musician said 'He plays rough like a man sharpening knives with yellow sand', but perhaps this comment reflected an element of professional jealousy rather than objective criticism.

It was the custom at this time for the gentlemen to escort their partners home, walking alongside the sedans with drawn swords. This was in spite of the filthy streets and, as it is delicately expressed in *Traditions of Edinburgh*, 'despite of all the sky-showers and land-showers which might be poured down on them at the pleasure of the powers above'.[25]

Not surprisingly, after running the gauntlet of the High Street, the gentlemen would return to the supper room to drink a toast to each and every lady until one of their number fell senseless to the floor.

Between 1746 and 1776 the Edinburgh Assembly Rooms were expanded and new directresses appointed. The Countesses of Leven, Glencairn and Hopetoun and Ladies Minto and Milntoun were amongst the new recruits. Later, the Honourable Miss Nicolas Murray, daughter of Viscount Stormont and sister of the Earl of Mansfield, was to become one of the best known directresses.

Miss Nicky Murray lived in a building at the head of Bailie Fife's Close in Edinburgh's High Street. She and her sisters were said to conduct a 'finishing establishment' for younger relatives from the country and her manner 'had all the bland and amiable gentleness of a downright arbitrary, feudal and undisputed sovereignty'.[26] Those who failed to meet her standards of birth and gentility were liable to be requested to leave the ballroom.

The task of directress was demanding and, at times, unenviable. Miss Nicky Murray so impressed Sir Alexander Boswell that he wrote:

> Order and elegance presided there;
> Each gay Right Honourable had her place
> To walk a Minuet with becoming grace.
> No racing to the dance with rival hurry;

Such was thy sway, O famed Miss Nicky Murray.
Each lady's fan a chosen Damon bore
With care selected many a day before.[27]

She remained one of the most outstanding directresses until her death in 1775, although she was remembered by some more for her good manners than her good nature.

Within the Assembly Rooms in Assembly Close sat Lord Kirkcudbright, a glover, who assumed his title in 1730 upon the death of a distant relation. (His son was granted the title legally in 1773.) He stood in the lobby selling gloves to the gentlemen who were required to have a new pair of white gloves every time they went to dance. Oliver Goldsmith sneered at this poor man in a letter to a friend: 'One day – happening to stop into Lord Kilcobry's – don't be surprised – his Lordship is only a glover!'[28]

The ballroom opened off a lobby at street level above which was a tea-room. The dancing room had a railed space in the centre within which the dancers were arranged while the spectators sat around on the outside. No communication was allowed between the different sides of this rail.

The dancing area was so small that it was Miss Murray's job to divide the dancers into sets, arranged in order of rank. Tickets were allotted to each set of ten to twelve couples and there was room for only one set at a time. The wide dresses and the pattern of the dances demanded the maximum possible space.

The pattern of a Minuet formed the letter Z. It was an 'open-couple' dance performed with tiny precise steps and a dainty, mannered air which echoed the style of the Georgian period.

Captain Topham, on his visit to Edinburgh, describes the routine. Couples were allotted to sets as soon as they arrived.

After this etiquette is over, the first Set dance Minuets beginning in the order of the tickets which are distributed by the Lady Directress, and then one Country Dance in the middle of the room which is surrounded by chairs to prevent the rest of the company from interfering with the dancers. At the conclusion of this, the second Set begins, and then the third and fourth in their respective turns till all the Sets have danced their Minuet and Country Dance.[29]

Meanwhile, the rest of the company sat and watched – ladies and their chaperones firmly segregated from the gentlemen.

In 1753 Oliver Goldsmith came to Edinburgh as a medical student and wrote sourly to his cousin:

When a stranger enters the dancing-hall, he sees one end of the room taken up by the ladies, who sit dismally in a group by themselves; in the other end stand their pensive partners that are to be; but no more intercourse between the sexes than there is between two countries at war. The ladies may ogle and the gentlemen sigh but an embargo is laid on any closer commerce.[30]

10

A minuet at the Assembly. Oliver Goldsmith may not have found this entertaining, but, from a female point of view, it offered an opportunity to dress up, chat to friends, assess the eligible men from a safe distance and take the centre stage at least once each evening. Sounds good to me!

Perhaps a young man straight from London, with no partner and no friends, might have failed to appreciate how much the ladies and gentlemen in Edinburgh were enjoying themselves.

Rules of behaviour were displayed on the wall for dancers to read and observe. They included clear strictures about dress.

> No lady to be admitted in a nightgown and no gentleman in boots; No misses in skirts and jackets, robecoats nor stay-bodied gowns to be allowed to dance Country Dances but in a Set by themselves.

(A nightgown was a kind of semi-evening dress, not quite formal enough for a ballroom.)

It was important that everyone should keep to the appointed position.

> It is expected no gentleman will step over the rail round the dancing place, but will enter or go out by the doors at the upper or lower end of the room; and that all ladies and gentlemen will order their servants not to enter the passage before the outer door with lighted flambeaux.[31]

In Edinburgh, assemblies began at precisely 4 pm in the winter and 6 pm in the summer. No dance could begin after 11 pm. At the stroke of eleven the directress indicated with her fan that musicians should stop playing and dancing should cease.

In Glasgow, ladies drew tickets for their places in one of the sets of 12 couples. Only two sets could dance a Country Dance at a time and no Reels were allowed without the permission of the director or directress. Rules about the behaviour of dancers were so explicit that they suggest the dancers were a lively group in need of firm discipline:

> No ladies to leave their place till the dance is finished.
> No ladies to stand up in the Country Dance except in the place to which their ticket entitles them and are requested to keep their ticket for the evening.
> When a lady has called one dance her place in the next is at the bottom of it.[32]

During the 1770s there had been a marked expansion of social life in Edinburgh and Glasgow. Dancing had become a respectable and accepted pastime even in the smaller towns and almost every town had its assembly room.

Large numbers of dancing teachers set up dancing schools in the cities and in 1775 Mr Topham remarked that there were more dancing teachers in Edinburgh than in any other city.[33] The Continental and, particularly, French influence in the Scottish capital was evident in the style of dancing taught. Dancing teachers proliferated as assemblies became more popular. Pupils learned a variety of French, English and Scottish dances including the Minuet and Country Dances, Cotillons and Allemandes. Amongst the dancing teachers of the time were: Mr MacQueen, Skinners' Close; Mr Strange, Todrick's Wynd; Mr Barnard, Skinners' Close; Mr Martin, Weir's Land; Mr Laurie, Todrick's Wynd; Signor Violanti, Monsieur D'Eggville and Madame Bonnet, Carruber's Close; and Charles le Picq, Skinners' Close.[34]

The Allemande was a circular dance in which the couples danced with intertwining arms held up at shoulder level. The Country Dance was a communal social dance, the basic form of which was partners facing each other in two lines as in Strip the Willow and The Haymakers. As the eighteenth century progressed, more Country Dances were devised to fit Scottish dance tunes and steps were modified to incorporate some favourite Scottish steps.

Growing more popular in the Lowlands was the Highland Reel. This was usually danced by two couples, and the figures differed slightly according to locality. The dancers stood face to face and when reeling described a figure of eight. Dancers all began at the same time instead of taking turns as in the country dances. Jigs, Hornpipes, Marches and Strathspeys added more variety to the dancers' repertoire. Unlike the restrained risings and fallings of the Minuet, Strathspeys were more reminiscent of the sixteenth century Galliard. The Edinburgh publisher, Creech, described the Reel as riotous and the Strathspey as sprightly.

The Cotillon, a French Contredance, was performed in a square with two couples standing at each side of the square facing inwards. It developed a great number of figures and eventually turned into a forfeit game in which kisses had to be given by ladies unable to execute certain figures. The calls for a Cotillon by the MC were not unlike the calls for an American Barn Dance almost two centuries later. 'Set to partners, ladies chain, promenade half round, half right and left, traversary, set to partners, half rights and lefts to places . . .'

Captain Topham was less than complimentary about the dancing in Scotland. Writing to a friend he said:

> The dances of this country are entirely devoid of grace . . . the general dance here is the Reel which requires that particular sort of step to dance properly, of which none but the people of the country can have any idea . . . the Scotch ladies . . . will sit totally unmoved at the most sprightly airs of an English Country Dance but the moment one of these [Reel] tunes is played . . . up they start, animated with new life, and you would imagine they had received an electrical shock or been bit by a tarantula.

He complained that the Scotsmen came to dance for exercise, hardly looked at their partners and would even take pleasure in Reels with four gentlemen instead of lady partners . . .

> Another of the national dances is a kind of quick minuet, or what the Scotch call a Strathspey. We in England are said to walk a minuet: this is gallopping a minuet.

On the other hand he had great admiration for the ladies:

> They conform themselves much more to the manners and taste of Paris with which they have as constant a communication as with England. The ladies in Edinburgh dress in general, with more elegance and in a way better accommodated to their persons, size and shape than most of the European nations . . . But I wish I could say as much for the men.[35]

Minutes of the Edinburgh Assembly end in 1776 and record that during the thirty years of High Street assemblies, more than £3,000 was donated to the Royal Infirmary, £3,000 to the Charity Workhouse and £1,500 to other charities.[36] This may explain how the dancers were able to silence the dissenting voices of authority who disapproved of dancing – for who could disapprove when the exercise was done in the name of charity?

As Edinburgh city grew in size and spread southwards new Assembly Rooms were built to accommodate the newcomers. Dancing was held for a while in a hall on the west side of Buccleuch Street owned by the Royal Company of Archers. Francis Bonnard was appointed manager of the Assemblies there. By 1785 Bonnard had transferred to the newly built George Square Assembly Rooms situated at 15 Buccleuch Place. All who proposed attending the assembly that winter were required to call at the Archers' Hall to sign the subscription paper. This assembly became very popular with the citizens who lived on the south side of the city.

In Lord Cockburn's opinion, 'The whole fashionable dancing, as indeed the fashionable anything, clung to George Square'. (The south side of George Square had not yet been built, which is why the Buccleuch Place venue was called the George Square Assembly).This Assembly was conducted in the traditional manner with a directress in charge of proceedings. Lord Cockburn records:

Lady Don and Mrs Rochhead of Inverleith both shone, first as hooped beauties and then as ladies of ceremonies. No couple could dance unless each party was provided with a ticket prescribing the precise place, in the precise dance . . . . If the ticket had marked upon it – say for a country dance, the figures 3.5; this meant that the holder was to place himself in the 3rd dance, and 5th from the top; and if he was anywhere else, he was set right, or excluded. Woe on the poor girl who with ticket 2.7, was found opposite a youth marked 5.9! It was flirting without a license, and looked very ill, and would probably be reported by the ticket director of that dance to the mother.[37]

Young Walter Scott, who was brought up in George Square, attended the George Square Rooms and danced there with his first love, Miss Williamina Belsches.

At George Square the managers also catered for children. A ball in 1789 began at 6 pm, when not only young people but others 'living in family with them' were invited. Mr Bayle took over from Mr Bonnard and under him assemblies continued there until the end of the century.

Despite increased acceptance of assemblies, the public still disapproved of masquerades, which were held to be occasions of wild debauchery under cover of fancy dress and masks. No doubt keen to test public opinion, Mr Digges, manager of the Theatre Royal in Edinburgh, devised and advertised on 22 February, 1775, a Grand Masked Ball to be held in the theatre. He promised:

the stage will be cleared and large columns wreathed with flowers and decorated with lustres ranged on each side so as to form an elegant saloon. A floor will be laid over the Pit to join it to the stage. And sideboards with refreshments will be opened for the company. Different, suitable paintings will embellish the whole room. None but persons in masked dresses will·be admitted.[38]

Now, who could resist that?

Unfortunately Mr Digges had misjudged the climate of opinion. Edinburgh was strongly opposed to the venture. Church leaders raised their voices in the pulpits once again. Three days after the first advertisement appeared, a new one took its place. Mr Digges had abandoned the scheme in favour of a grand Ridotto. Dancers would wear fancy dress but no masks and the evening still included the provision of musical entertainment and food – a kind of latter-day dinner/dance with cabaret. The wisdom of his decision was confirmed when the evening turned out to be a tremendous success. It was recorded on 11 March 1775: 'There never was in this kingdom an entertainment conducted with more elegance and decorum'. You can't say fairer than that!

Alongside these new diversions, Edinburgh society continued to attend more traditional entertainments. Comely Gardens had long been a popular meeting place in which to dance and take decorous leafy walks during the summer months in what was a pale imitation of the famous Vauxhall Gardens in London. In 1784 a ballroom was opened at Comely Gardens but it seemed to find little favour. As the century progressed it was condemned by the smart set as commonplace and slow. Hugo Arnot described it as 'a wretched attempt to imitate Vauxhall for which neither the climate nor the gardens are adapted.'[39]

More popular was the ballroom opened in 1776 at Ranelach Garden, Kirkbraehead by Signor Corri. (Kirkbraehead was a small village set between present day Rutland Street and Lynedoch Place). Possibly the situation to the west of the city explains the need for gimmicks. The garden was illuminated 'with transparent machinery and upwards of four hundred lamps of various kinds'.[40] The ballroom was illuminated with spermaceti candles and the programme was to include a musical entertainment lasting two hours. As the annual subscription was a guinea this seemed to offer splendid value.

Other ballrooms were being opened all the time. In Edinburgh there were new hotels in the New Town, each with a magnificent ballroom; there were new Assembly Rooms in Leith; and for grand occasions such as Hunters' Balls there was Holyroodhouse itself.

Edinburgh was growing rapidly now as the opening of the North Bridge gave access to the New Town. Arnot wrote in 1779:

> A new house for holding Assemblies is much needed in Edinburgh. In the present one the dancing is neither elegant nor commodious. There are two tea or card rooms but no supper room. A table is covered in the dancing room before the company meets . . . after dancing, extra tables and chairs are brought in while the company waits.[41]

It seemed that the citizens of Edinburgh agreed with him. In 1781 a committee, presided over by the Earl of Moray, examined the problem. A circular was produced by the managers of the assembly to support the idea of a new building:

> It will remove the reproach that many a market town in England has a more elegant Assembly Room than the capital of Scotland; by rendering these amusements more elegant it will improve and polish the manners of society, and independent of the two great considerations of health and safety, it is believed the preservation of ladies' dresses which suffer such destruction in the present incommodious Rooms, will of itself be the equivalent for the charge of the undertaking.[42]

Under such a barrage of argument, in which could be detected a strong feminine influence, the town council was completely won over. The promoters were given as much ground in George Street in the New Town as they required at a cost of one thousand and three pounds, seven shillings and nine pence. The foundation stone was laid in May 1783 and the building completed in 1786 at the cost of 600 guineas. The magnificent new ballroom, ninety-two feet long by forty-two feet wide and forty feet high, had two side rooms known as the East and West servant's waiting rooms. Here the bearers of the sedan chairs awaited their mistresses' pleasure. They gathered round the fireplaces and enjoyed a convivial evening until they were required to provide transport home. A tea-room fifty feet by thirty-six was to serve as a ballroom on ordinary occasions and a grand

The elegance of the new Assembly Rooms in Edinburgh has survived, and the exterior remains almost unchanged in 1994

saloon, thirty-eight feet by forty-four feet all combined to be among the most elegant ballrooms in Britain, according to the *Edinburgh Advertiser* of April 1783.

The gentlemen of the Caledonian Hunt held the first ball there on 11 January 1787. Captain Graham was MC and the function was attended by 340 dancers including 'all the people of fashion in town. The dresses of the ladies in different colours of satin set off by Spanish or turban-style hats were in the highest state of taste and elegance'. Reporters of the day declared, however, 'the dress of the gentlemen was in no way remarkable'.[43] Supper was at 2 am. Ladies retired about 4 am and 'the morning was pretty far advanced before the gentlemen left'. In these new surroundings, Country Dances now ousted the Minuet and some new rules were introduced:

> No young gentleman with unpowdered or untied hair, wearing boots or carrying cane to be admitted. No young lady out of woman's dress allowed to dance.[44]

It seems that the keynote for dancing in Edinburgh was elegance.

In Glasgow, the assemblies had become established in the new Assembly Rooms in Ingram Street. This was a grand three-storey building decorated with four Ionic columns and with a ballroom eighty feet long, thirty-five feet wide and twenty-seven feet high. (The old rooms in the Tontine were smaller – forty-seven feet by twenty-seven feet by twenty-four feet). In keeping with the grander style, there were two musicians' galleries at each end of the ballroom and two marble

The Glasgow Assembly Rooms in Ingram Street, where the first assembly was held on 18 January 1798. The Rooms were demolished in the 1890s to make way for an extension to the GPO, but the wings survived until 1911. The central section of the frontage was transformed into a triumphal arch at the south end of Charlotte Street

chimney pieces with large mirrors above the mantels. As in Edinburgh, dances were held weekly during the winter season. The opening assembly was held on 18 January, 1798, in honour of Her Majesty the Queen Charlotte's birthday. Tickets normally costing four shillings were raised to five shillings on that occasion. Mrs Kennedy presided as directress and the 'uncommonly brilliant company' numbered 350 ladies and gentlemen. By 1799 there was a record of an attendance of 460 dancers.

At the end of the eighteenth century, dancing was firmly established in Scotland, particularly in the two cities of Edinburgh and Glasgow, as a popular pastime for the wealthy and titled. The number of dancers had risen so fast that it was necessary to have custom-built assembly rooms, often with ancillary rooms for supper and card-playing. Accommodation had to be found for dancers, chaperones, musicians, servants and sedan chairs. Space was required for the voluminous dresses in vogue and, as the fashion for dancing continued to spread, there was a growing preference for more lively dances. The spirit of the age was for revolution and change. The eighteenth century had seen the Union of Parliaments, the 1745 Jacobite Rebellion, the American War of Independence, the French Revolution (which killed off the Minuet in France along with the aristocrats), and the Industrial Revolution.

In this atmosphere young dancers had little patience for the slow Minuet and were ready for the excitement of a new dance. It was just on the horizon.

CHAPTER TWO

Popular Assemblies

ോ ഔ

The Nineteenth Century

The nineteenth century saw two marked changes in ballroom dancing. The first change was on the social level. As Britain changed from an agricultural to a more industrial society, the growth of the merchant or middle classes put pressure on the assemblies to set aside the strict class barriers.

A complaint in a newspaper in 1812 shows an early trend towards ballroom equality: 'In 1772 silk stockings were used only by gentlemen and that on great occasions; now all ranks have them, no lady can be dressed without them, nor any Miss for a boarding school ball.'[1]

In Paris it was claimed that by 1789 there were nearly 700 dance halls. The start of the new century saw dance halls and assemblies proliferating in large towns like London, Epsom, Bath, and Tunbridge Wells. In Edinburgh and Glasgow regular assemblies flourished while smaller Scottish towns held assemblies in local halls.

The smaller towns were first to open assemblies to a wider social range, while as late as 1880 Edinburgh was still experimenting with ways of restricting admission. There was an attempt to operate a voucher system. These vouchers could only be purchased from patronesses who were therefore able to restrict them to the socially acceptable. When this proved unmanageable, the assemblies switched to a more open system of subscriptions which were usually purchased from a nearby shop. Anyone with the means to pay the subscription could now attend the assemblies.

The second major change came with the introduction of new dances. Until now, the strongest influence on ballroom dancing was French. The Minuet, Allemande, and Contredances stemmed from the French court as did the Ecossaise – a French dance with no Scottish connections despite its name. The Ecossaise was very similar to English Country Dances but was more energetic, and danced at a faster tempo, often to Scottish tunes.

However, having emerged from the French Revolution in 1793, at the start of the nineteenth century France was plunged into the Napoleonic Wars. It is not surprising to find that, with political revolution in the air, a similar mood affected the dances in the ballroom.

The most influential of the new dances was not French in origin. The Waltz arrived amid public outcry. This circular dance excited shock and scandal because of the hold which entitled gentlemen to 'embrace' their partners round the waist. In previous dances partners were linked more distantly by hand or arm. (The earlier Allemande had introduced the idea of a circular dance but the hold was not so close.)

The Waltz probably had its roots in the 'turning dances' in Germany, although there were some similarities in the Italian Volta. Turning figures had been prominent in German dances since the fifteenth century and in Nuremburg, it was said that the turning became so prolonged and so furious that women were taken out of the dance dizzy and fainting, and the dance was outlawed.

By this time many ballroom floors had acquired a high polish and many were laid in parquet. This enabled the dancers to move faster and to glide over the floor, which in turn had some influence on the style of the new dances.[2] Instructions for preparing floors were given in *Woman's Life* magazine:

To prepare a floor for dancing, have it well washed and when the boards are thoroughly dry, scatter boracic powder over them and rub it well with the feet . . . children in the house can slide on the boards lengthwise. Or, after it is dry, rub the floor over with milk.

The Waltz had been scandalising Europe since the mid-eighteenth century but steadily gained favour, especially in France immediately after the Revolution.

In Britain, the Waltz was first seen officially at the London ballroom, 'Almack's', in 1812. (The fashionable Almack's was built by a Scot, William Almack who came from Galloway. It opened in February 1765.) Following the demonstration of the new dance, it was claimed that 'no event ever produced so great a sensation in English society.'[3]

Despite sporadic attacks from the press, the Waltz gained popularity and, finally, official sanction from Queen Charlotte and the Prince Regent when it was included in a ball at Carlton House on 12 July 1816. The *Times* reported, 'The dancing consisted only of Waltzing and Cotillons, in which none of the Royal Family joined.' On 16 July, 1816, the *Times* continued: 'We remarked with pain that the indecent foreign dance called the Waltz was introduced (we believe for the first time) at the English Court on Friday last. This is a circumstance which ought not to be passed over in silence. National morals depend on national habits . . .'[4]

Lord Byron was so scandalised that he wrote a poem, 'The Waltz – an Apostrophic Hymn':

WALTZING OF THE PERIOD.

The Lady Honoria D———, as she appeared taking leave of her Mamma, previous to going into action.

The Lady Honoria as she appeared when the engagement was over.

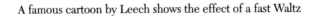

A famous cartoon by Leech shows the effect of a fast Waltz

Say – would you wish to make those beauties quite so cheap?
Hot from the hands promiscuously applied,
Round the slight waist or down the glowing side . . .[5]

And he returned to the subject in 'English Bards and Scotch Reviewers':

Now round the room the circling dow'gers sweep,
Now in loose waltz the thin-clad daughters leap;
The first in lengthened line majestic swim
The last display the free unfetter'd limb!
Those for Hibernia's lusty sons repair
With art the charms which nature could not spare
Those after husbands wing their eager flight
Nor leave much mystery for the nuptial night.[6]

The Waltz was too popular for these criticisms to have much effect and the music of Joseph Lanner, Johann Strauss the elder and his son, Johann Strauss ('the Waltz King' famous for 'The Blue Danube') only served to increase its popularity. (Other composers who became noted for their Waltz music were Weber, Chopin, Brahms, Schumann and Lehar). By the time Queen Victoria came to the throne in 1837 all opposition was overthrown and the Waltz was firmly established.

In some early Waltzes, couples formed a circle round the room and performed the dance to music that was fast and energetic. However, later the music slowed and couples were no longer confined to a circle but could dance freely across the floor. Waltz tempos varied and the famous Viennese Waltz was one of the fastest. Some claim that Weber, with his famous piano piece, 'The Invitation to the Dance' composed in 1819, laid down the ideal speed.

A writer in the *Woman's Life* magazine of 1896 worked out the surprising distances involved in an evening's dancing:

During a waltz you would go six times round a moderate sized ballroom making, say, a circuit of 80 yards, That is 480 yards if you went in line, but you are turning around once each yard which will bring each waltz to over three quarters of a mile or at least 14 miles for the 18 waltzes.

The Waltz introduced a new rhythm of 3/3 time – strong, weak, weak. One writer claims that 'The Waltz is basically a work rhythm. It was the first work rhythm that we ever accepted above the level of folk dance . . . .Try swinging a pick to a Minuet and you won't get much work done, but you can swing a pick splendidly to a Waltz.'[7]

The rhythm of the Waltz was infectious. The development of a slight hesitation before the strong beat – strong, weak, hesitate – most noticeable in the Viennese Waltz, gave a tension and an excitement to the dance.

Another newcomer that became an immediate success in Scotland was the

Quadrille – a form of square dance which had endless variations. The Quadrille was a French dance which came directly to Scotland from Paris in 1816 after the Napoleonic wars. The dancing teacher Barclay Dun published a book in Edinburgh in 1818 entitled *Quadrilles* in which he enthused: 'No kind of dancing is so well fitted for society as the Quadrille . . . it admits of breathing time and gives an opportunity for conversation to those of the set who are disengaged.' Dancers of Quadrilles, he said, 'should glide like skaters with smoothness and softness'.[8]

The arrangement of dancers in a Quadrille was a square formation with the first couple facing the third and the second couple facing the fourth. Figures were generally begun by the first couple.

The Lancers followed the appearance of the Quadrille later in the century. These two were the last stages of the communal dance. The older Country Dance (the French Contredance), which was danced in the Scottish Lowlands, had a linear form in which the figures were generally started by the top couple. Typical of these were 'Strip the Willow' and 'The Haymakers'.

The one truly Scottish dance had a different form. In the Reel, dancers began all at the same time and formed a kind of chain. In the first half of the century Scottish Country Dancing had become fashionable, perhaps encouraged by Queen Victoria's love of things Scottish.

Other dances gaining popularity were the Circassian Circle, Waltz Country Dance, and the Dashing White Sergeant. The kissing dance was a favourite – variously known as Bee-Baw-Babbity, Babbity Bowster or the White Cockade. In the Circassian Circle ladies progressed round the room exchanging partners as they went which made this a very good mixing dance. The Dashing White Sergeant combined the idea of a progressive Country Dance with the steps of a Reel and was another good 'mixer'.

While very popular with the young, these dances scandalised parents as the Cotillon had done a century before. A father's letter to the agony column of the *Spectator* as early as 1711 gives a fair idea of the way many parents reacted both south and north of the Border:

My eldest daughter, a girl of sixteen, has for some time been under the tuition of Monsieur Rigadoon, a Dancing Master in the City; and I was prevailed upon by her and her mother to go last night to one of his balls . . . I must acquaint you that very great abuses are crept into this entertainment. I was amazed to see my girl handed by, and handing young fellows with so much familiarity; and I could not have thought it had been in the child. They very often made use of a most impudent and lascivious step called 'Setting', which I know not how to describe to you, but by telling you that 'tis the very reverse of 'Back to Back'. At last an impudent young dog bid the fiddlers to play a dance called Moll Pately, and after having made two or three capers, ran to his partner, locked his arms in hers, and whisked her round cleverly above ground in such a manner, that I, who sat upon one of the lowest benches, saw further above her shoe than I think fit to acquaint you with.

The reply offered small comfort.

I must confess I am afraid that my correspondent had too much reason to be a little out of humour at the treatment of his daughter, but I conclude that he might have been much more so had he seen one of those kissing dances in which, Will Honeycomb assures me, they are obliged to dwell almost a minute on the fair one's lips or they will be too quick for the music and the dance quite out of time . . .[9]

In other words, there was no point in complaining. It could have been worse!

For more formal affairs there was the Polonaise, a processional dance and one of the national dances of Poland, introduced in 1830. It was, in fact, a version of a much older dance dating back to about 1573 when nobles took their wives by the hand and made them parade before King Henry of Anjou, stepping in rhythm and displaying their dresses.

The Galop was rarely seen outside Hunt Balls and private parties and never achieved general popularity. It was an extremely simple dance in which the gentleman placed his right arm lightly round his partner's waist and with the other held her right hand. The couples faced out towards their line of direction round the room and proceeded by means of chassés and turns.

One dance that did become established quickly was the Polka. It originated in Czechoslovakia, and first appeared in England in 1844 achieving immediate fantastic popularity. It was another close-couple dance but livelier than the Waltz.

The Paris correspondent of the *Times* commented in March 1844: 'Our private letters state that politics are for the moment suspended in public regard by the

Example of a dance programme from a later period. Both ladies and gentlemen had to fill in a card so as to remember their partners for each dance

new and all-absorbing pursuit – the Polka . . . which embraces in its qualities the intimacy of the Waltz and the vivacity of the Irish Jig'.[10]

It was so appealing that some dance programmes could include six Polkas in the course of an evening. This dance was to continue to attract dancers for the rest of the century. In 1886 George Grossmith wrote the hit music, 'See me Dance the Polka', which was to become the tune most associated with the dance. The Polka was the dance that brought about the introduction of 'Tea Dances' which came into vogue in England in 1845.

By this period many public halls and salons were lit by gas following the example of the Prince Regent who had arranged for the Royal Pavilion in Brighton to be the first gas-lit ballroom in Britain in 1845. He also had the Buckingham Palace ballroom re-conditioned for Queen Victoria, installing 540 gas lights with the illumination of 10,000 candle power. Towards the end of the century a few private owners had begun to light their ballrooms with the very latest form of power – electricity.

Another new dance in the ballrooms, the Schottische in 1849, was followed by the more successful Highland Schottische in 1855. This was of German origin and is a slower dance than the Polka but with similar music. The American Barn Dance arrived in Britain in 1888. The name came from the first tune it was danced to: 'Dancing in the Barn'. Following the establishment of the British Association of Teachers of Dancing, which was founded in 1892, an annual competition was held to discover a new sequence dance. The Veleta was an entry by Mr Arthur Morris of Leeds. His entry failed to win the prize but the dance was taken up afterwards and was destined to figure in dancing programmes for many years. It consisted of simple figures performed sometimes side by side and some-times facing each other followed by a gliding movement and a few bars of a Waltz.

In Scotland, the newer dances tended to appear first in the cities of Glasgow and Edinburgh while the more traditional dancing further north was slower to change. This was no reflection on the attitudes to dance across the country but was more likely the result of the difficulties of communication outwith the main cities. J F and T M Flett describe the pattern of dances throughout this period:

> In the Lowlands, the introduction of the various Square Dances and Circle Dances in the first half of the nineteenth century had only temporary effects on the popularity of the already established Reels and Country Dances, and effectively the new dances were simply assimilated into the existing dance programmes. After about 1870, however, the Square Dances and Circle Dances began to oust Reels and Country Dances from the dance programmes in the larger Lowland towns and by 1900 the pro-grammes in these places consisted almost entirely of Square Dances and Circle Dances together with an occasional Scotch Reel and a few Country Dances such as Petronella, Flowers of Edinburgh, Rory o' More and Strip the Willow.[11]

Professional dance teachers could be found in almost every town and many travelled to outlying districts as everyone was eager to learn to dance. Dancing lessons were seen as an essential part of Scottish social life since dancing teach-ers also taught manners and deportment along with the dance steps.

In Dundee, D Anderson's 'Ballroom Guide' described in detail 'Thirteen sets of quadrilles, nineteen circle and miscellaneous dances and upwards of sixty original and selected Country Dances.' It also included hints on etiquette and dress.[12]

The growth of popular ballroom dancing in Dundee is typical of many small towns in Scotland. In 1802 an assembly was held in the Trades Hall in honour of Her Majesty Queen Charlotte's birthday, and 150 dancers were present. In 1809 a series of dances was held in the Town Hall, but there were complaints of shortage of space. There was a move to the Exchange Coffee Rooms, which could hold 300, and there was a Grand Masquerade and Fancy Ball there in 1820. The first of its kind in Dundee, it was described as eminently successful, although the reporter commented wryly that in such a small town where everyone knew everyone the wearing of masks was insufficient disguise!

James Watson's Annual Ball in Dundee was held in the Caledonian Hall in Castle Street in 1824. (James Watson's claim to fame was that he could play three instruments at once.)

In 1830 an important change was recorded. 'The separation of gentry of town and country in balls and Assemblies has been amicably adjusted'. The first 'Union Ball' took place in the Town Hall, marking the removal of one social barrier.

In the larger and more sophisticated city of Edinburgh, dancing was now on a much grander scale and larger numbers took part. However, an anonymous contemporary writer seemed to suggest that some dancers still preferred the older premises:

> George Square Assembly Rooms are sufficient elegant and commodious and the subscription assemblies in them have been for some time rather preferred by fashionable company to the dancing assemblies in George Street in the New Town.[13]

Certainly, Walter Scott danced in the George Square Assemblies which were so conveniently close to his family home.

The visit of George IV to Edinburgh on 26 August 1822 called for the grandest possible arrangements. The king had decided that he would be the first Hanoverian monarch to visit Scotland. Sir Walter Scott was in charge of the reception and chiefs and clansmen were summoned to appear in full regalia. Two balls were held in George Street Assembly Rooms during the visit, one by the Caledonian Hunt and another by the Peers of Scotland. A throne hung with rich crimson velvet was placed at the east end of the ballroom but the King preferred to mingle with the company and refused to occupy it.

The story is told that at the Hunt Ball, Nathaniel Gow, son of the famous Neil Gow (and author of the song, 'Caller Herrin'), was playing the violin.

> In the course of the evening he played his own composition, 'Wha'll be King but Charlie' – not the most tactful choice in front of a monarch whose grandfather had

defeated Charles Edward Stuart in 1745! He rendered the tune so well that the King went over and asked the name of the tune. 'Wha'll be King but Charlie,' said Gow, to the no small embarrassment of the assembled guests within hearing. His Majesty requested Gow to play it over again, and on more than one subsequent occasion of a like nature ordered that this particular tune should be included in the programme.[14]

A painting of the royal visit to the ballroom is ascribed to Turner and the original is held by the Tate Gallery in London.

Two years later, in 1824, fire destroyed the older ballroom in Old Assembly Close but it did nothing to restrain the local enthusiasm for dancing.

Hunt Balls became the accepted entry into society for debutantes. Eleanor Sillar describes how in 1887 at the age of eighteen she was launched into society at the Hunt Ball in the Assembly Rooms. A French dressmaker designed her gown – white silk with silver bugled net for draperies – and her nursemaid helped her with the tight corsets then in fashion. Escorted by her brother, she travelled by cab to George Street. In her long-white-gloved hands she clasped a white fan and a bouquet of lily of the valley. Her evening coat was an Indian shawl pattern and a cloud of net protected her coiled-up hair.

In the dressing room she met her chaperone, Mrs Brown, and along with other debutantes and chaperones she was led into the ballroom. Dance cards were filled in, and to the music of Dambman's Band the girls whirled off into the dance. The programme included Waltzes, Lancers, Polkas, Eightsome Reels, Strathspeys, the Reel of Tulloch and a final D'ye ken John Peel.

Eleanor describes the evening:

Waltz! Waltz! Lancers! not yet the kitchen kind, graceful and gay. A Polka! whirl and spring, down the whole length of the room on one side, up the other, hand in hand, hopping and skipping, laughing. 'For a romping rollicking Polka is the jolliest fun I know!' blares the band. A pause; then the Reel. This is serious. The Eightsome circles form, there is a bit of fussing about the right people for the right set. We wait, hands linked, arms at full stretch. A chord, then the full-throated yell which starts us off on a twenty minute madness. But a madness with a method in it, for here are Highland names and Highland blood, so, no fooling! I note with awe the rapt expression on my partner's face. His eyes gaze into space, then on once more; the Strathspey, the Reel of Tulloch. Wilder the yells, our feet seem on springs. Then a long last enthusiastic chord, and the band sinks back and mops its brow. Loud clappings come from the serried ranks on the raised seats. Breathless, reluctant, a trifle dishevelled, from delirious heights we drop again to the quiet levels of civilised behaviour. My partner bows, I curtsey and my hand in his arm we seek supper . . .[15]

The *Evening Dispatch* lists the programme of dances in the Edinburgh Assembly Rooms in 1845. There were eleven sets of Quadrilles, five Waltzes, four Polkas (which had become extremely popular here the previous year) and four Reels.

Towards the end of the nineteenth century dancing was less popular in England. After the death of Prince Albert in 1861 Queen Victoria withdrew from public life and, for the first time, good dancing became unfashionable. However, this attitude did not necessarily extend to Scotland. Highland balls proliferated throughout the nineteenth century, setting a precedent which continues to this day. The annual ball at Blair Castle, the home of the Duke of Atholl, began officially when the new ballroom was added to the castle in 1877. Nathaniel Gow was in charge of the music there. A plaque on the wall of Gow's cottage at Inver, near Dunkeld, bears witness to his excellence in the words of the national poet, Burns:

> Nae fabled wizard's wand I trow
> Had e'er the magic art o' Gow.

In Skye, the Skye Gathering held in 1876 was intended to encourage Highland dancing and the wearing of Highland dress, since the repeal of the Act of Proscription in 1781 was apparently not enough to persuade people back into their traditional garb.

Dunvegan Castle was also host to a Highland ball, as were the big houses of Traquair and Hopetoun. The Traquair diaries of Mary Ravenscroft, wife of the 7th Earl of Traquair, give details of the dancing master, Mr Harper, engaged to teach her daughter, Louisa. Hopetoun House boasted one of the largest private ballrooms in Scotland. Its length was 100 feet and it was 30 feet high. It could take four sets of dancers across the floor.

Max O'Rell, writing in 1887, describes the dancing scene in Scotland at the time:

> In Scotland, people still dance. The Scotch have preserved the primitive, innocent, pastoral character of this exercise. Nothing is more graceful than the Reel and Schottische of the Highlands . . . Ask me how Society dances in Scotland and I will answer: just as it does elsewhere, but with a gravity that would do honour to our senators.
>
> The Scotch are not all agreed as to whether dancing is sinful or not. Certain dwellers in the Highlands look on it as the eighth deadly sin: the Shakers on the contrary, consider it as the most edifying of religious exercises. Between the two the margin is wide.
>
> If I am to believe the Scotch with whom I have talked on the subject, it is not dancing that they object to, it is the fashion in which people dance nowadays. They admire the Contredance and Minuet but consider it improper that a man should whirl round a room with a half-dressed lady in his arms.[16]

The nineteenth century was one of changing fashions in dance but it also saw radical changes in dress. For men the greatest change was from knee breeches to trousers. The trousers which appeared in 1815 were to go through various modifications in shape before they settled down to the basic narrow leg shape. At the beginning of the century, men's coats were cut away sharply in front and had wide lapels and deep collars. Their waistcoats were short and square-cut. Later on, the tail coat developed into the informal lounge suit which was the fore-runner of the suit of today. For formal evening functions evening dress was required.[17]

The hooped dresses of the ladies which were in vogue at the start of the century became long and clinging about 1820 with slim skirts and a high waist-line – the famous Empire line. Huge elaborate hair styles were reduced to man-ageable curls, often piled on top of the head. Five years later the dresses had become shorter and flounced out from the waist, usually with the aid of whale-bones. In the 1830s materials for evening dresses were China drape, Persian silks, light cashmeres, French tulle and organdie worn over white rayed muslin. There were balloon sleeves and pointed waists. By the 1850s the crinolene was popular with wide, sometimes double skirts and as many as a dozen starched pet-ticoats under a ball gown. A lady could not sit down for fear of crushing the starch. From 1868 onwards, skirts gradually became narrower with a bird-cage bustle attached. The Polonaise (upper skirt and bodice combined) was the thing to wear, often with a skirt of one colour and the Polonaise of another. Young girls preferred white or biscuit over pale blue or pink. Matrons preferred richly embroidered Polonaises with silk or Irish poplin or black satin quilted under-skirts. (Machine stitching became very popular in the early seventies.)

1875 brought the 'pin back', followed by the Princess robe which was long with a train, and tight to follow the lines of the body. The final years of the century gave way to the influence of the Aesthetic movement. There were no corsets; soft flowing 'greenery yallery hues' and faded pinks, greens and blues were in favour. Dress reform emphasised beauty and comfort. Evening nets, chiffons and lace over contrasting silk foundations were held to be in the greatest taste.

If all these changes in dress and dance were radical they were nothing com-pared to the changes on the way in the twentieth century. There were a few pointers to the new direction dancing was to take.

In 1894, Mr Edward Humphrey, of the Cavendish Rooms in London, started a monthly magazine which was destined to be the major magazine for ballroom dancers throughout the next century. It was called *The Dancing Times*. Even more significant was the opening of new ballrooms in the Mecca for ballroom dancers – Blackpool. In August 1894, the Tower Ballroom opened, to be fol-lowed by the Empress Ballroom in the Winter Gardens in 1897.

Another ballroom opened as the Alhambra but changed its name in 1904 to the Palace. This ballroom boasted the installation of a lift. The local press explained, 'Instead of going up the steps . . . you step inside a car, someone touches a button, and the apparatus does the rest.' Sir W H Bailey gave the inau-gural speech, reported in the local press, in which he praised the enterprise. He said that attention to amusement was just as important as the serious work of life; and handsome buildings such as this were not too good but rather tended to the elevation of the taste of the great class of people who demanded amusement. There were, within sixty miles of the town, eight millions of people who worked with intellect. For this class, amusement had to be provided and places like the Alhambra could not fail to be a service to the working classes.

No doubt the worthy gentleman had put his finger on the reason for the rise of large public ballrooms but he had no way of knowing how they would spread across the country nor that the Blackpool ballrooms were to become the ballroom equivalent of Wimbledon.

Perhaps the most significant pointer to change came with the arrival of two new dances at the end of the century, not from France or Europe but from America. The Washington Post was a two-step danced to lively and novel music. It resembled a double-quick march with a skip in each step done as rapidly as a couple could go forward, backward and turn.

The Cakewalk came from the American South where negro slaves had adapted the movements of the war dances of the Seminole Indians. As the dance was taken up by the smart set in America there were competitions for the best dancers and prizes of cakes were awarded, giving rise to the saying 'that takes the cake'.[18] By the time the dance reached New York the prizes were champion belts for the best male walkers and diamond rings for the women. The dance developed into a style of wild jumping and gyrating followed by slow processions.

As a dance it was not destined to last but it was important because it gave a strong hint of what was to come in the new century – Ragtime!

CHAPTER THREE

Growth of the Dancing Schools

ᏝᏬ ᏬᏬ

1900 to 1910

Before the new dances could take hold, some old attitudes had to change. Queen Victoria had loved dancing with Prince Albert, but as already mentioned, after his death in 1861 her prolonged mourning period had a profound effect on dancing even north of the Border. That is not to say that dancing stopped. What was frowned upon was any sign of enjoyment of dancing in public. In smart society there was no enthusiasm for dance and it was said that it was not good form for a young man to dance too well.

However, public dancing still continued under the guise of 'education'. Dancing teachers began to open 'academies' of dance in which they built their own ballrooms. Dancing was advocated as healthy exercise and a wonderful training ground for learning the rules of etiquette.

Examples of the prescriptive style of the period can be found in the Etiquette pages of *Women's Life* magazine:

> There is a new idea to design dance-cards with miniature paintings appropriate for the particular hop . . . white, light blue or pink, oblong with rounded corners . . . Some ladies giving a ball purchase programmes with hand painted designs at one shilling to two shillings and sixpence per programme. Pencils are purpose-made . . . twopence to sixpence each with ends of ivory, mother of pearl or gold.

and:

> Trains, long, floating veils, wings and similar adjuncts are apt in a crowd to become entangled in the spurs or swords or helmets of other dancers thereby reducing the wearers to despair or untidiness. Better far to choose something trim and smart of sufficient strength to resist the effects of romping through the Lancers.

When Edward VII came to the throne in 1902, attitudes were inclined to be authoritarian in polite society. This was a secure, orderly world where chaperones were still considered to be necessary for young ladies in public places such as dance halls. In some ways, dancing was stratified socially as much as ever. The difference was that now class distinction was shown by where, how and what you danced. Possession of rank or title meant restriction to a limited number of State or society balls while the middle and working classes enjoyed an increasingly wide choice of places and times to dance in public. The result of this was that ultimately the best dancers would come from the middle and working classes who had more opportunity to practise. The cream of society attended State Balls where they danced Quadrilles and Polkas, Waltzes and Galops. Waltzes were fast at about 50 bars a minute.

There were also private society dances in mansion houses and castles; and County Balls or Hunt Balls in Assembly Rooms. In these, Lancers and Two-steps were added to the programmes.

At another level there were Subscription dances where groups paid a subscription for admission to a set number of dances in the season. Dance programmes here were similar to the society dances but did not include the Galop.

Finally there were the assemblies of the dance teachers and a growing number of public assemblies where Quadrilles, Lancers, Cotillons and Waltzes (here, a slow 32 bars a minute) remained the most popular dances.

Up to 1910 the main attraction still lay in the steps of a dance. The teaching of dancing was based on the five positions of the feet with the feet pointed out as in ballet. Movements were artificial and 'pretty'.

The Scots, accustomed to the intricacies of traditional Reels and Country Dances, flocked to learn the steps of the more 'modern' dances. In the first years of the century people all over Scotland attended dancing classes. Some teachers travelled over a wide area to give dancing lessons in country districts. In Glasgow, where the population had exploded from 12,000 in 1708 to 731,675 in 1898, there were four big dance schools which were established by James Orr Robertson, Joe Diamond, James B MacEwan and J D MacNaughton. Another school, destined to become one of the most famous dancing schools in the city, the Warren Academy of Dancing, was opened on 30 May 1905 by John Warren in a basement at 285 Bath Street. In the early years he concentrated on Quadrille Assemblies and taught Old Time and Sequence Dancing. He held dances three nights a week on the upper floor and soon extended this to six nights a week – the first ballroom in the country to do that.

John Warren, senior, and his wife, Annie, who came originally from Falkirk, brought up four children – Alex, John, Anne and Jessie. At first the family had a flat in the basement of the school and their son John was actually born there – the equivalent of being born in a trunk in the Princess Theatre!

Edinburgh also had large dancing schools. Amongst the best-known was the school run by Mr D G MacLennan who later claimed to have brought the Fox-Trot to Britain. He was a multi-discipline dancer who taught ballroom, ballet,

The Warren family in 1908. Left to right: Annie Warren, baby Anne, John Warren snr., Alex, Jessie and John jnr.

stage and Highland dancing. (Originally a fine Highland dancer, he learned ballroom dancing from his brother, William). He also travelled as far as Skye to teach.

Macdonald's School of Dancing began in Valleyfield Street, Tollcross, and later moved to Pitt Street in Leith. It was ruled with a rod of iron by Mr Macdonald who used to announce at the start of the evening that if any gentleman lifted a lady so high that both her feet were off the floor, he would be ejected. There was a firm understanding that in the Lancers, dancers should always have one foot on the floor. In this formal setting, dancers were required to wear white gloves. Families would enrol for lessons and at the end of each evening there was always a Moonlight Waltz when young people were expected to invite their parents to dance.

Another typical dancing school in Edinburgh was Glendinning's. Grandfather William started to teach dancing in 1893 in Warrender Park Road. With his wife, two daughters and a son, he moved to 11 Pilrig Street in 1902 where they built a dance hall above the house. Their son, Andrew, continued the dancing tradition and his daughter, Dorothy, was born in Pilrig Street – another child born to dance. Dorothy was often called away from her school homework to make up a set in the ballroom or to sweep it out ready for the next pupils. No formal qualifications were required then to be a dancing teacher. (Dorothy was sixteen when the Imperial College in London introduced formal qualifications for teachers in 1926.) Later the family bought another large house at 1 Chalmers Crescent and the school flourished in the two centres for many years.

It was customary for teachers to advertise their classes in the local newspaper under the heading of Tuition. A typical advert in the Edinburgh *Evening News* in February 1900 read:

Mr and Miss Glendinning give lessons (class or private) in a fashionable ballroom – fancy dancing.
Practice Wed/Sat at 8 – splendid floor – electric light –
1 Chalmers Crescent.[1]

The Dunedin was yet another school. Situated near the top of Leith Walk, it was run by Danny Hanley and his wife who always insisted on leading off the dances. Later it was to be known as the Dunedin Palais.

In 1910 one small dancing school, Hunter's Academy in Newhaven Road, received its youngest and keenest pupil. Aged four, young Ena Linton persuaded the teacher, Miss Harding, to take her on. Ena took lessons and became the star pupil there for the next eight years. She recalled that on her first day Miss Harding wore a green satin dress and had a big feather in her hat. Her own dress was white and she wore white hand-knitted stockings and bronze dance shoes. She was a natural dancer and destined to dance for the rest of her working life.

In the rural towns round Dundee, Mr David Anderson taught ballroom dancing from 1870 to his death in 1907. He held classes in places like Brechin, Broughty Ferry and Tayport. Mr Anderson was the author of 'D Anderson's Ballroom and Solo Dance Guide – with Full Tuition in the Art of Dancing without the Use of French Terms'. He advertised:

All the latest Improvements and Newest Dances besides the Figures of all the Popular Quadrilles, Contra-Dances, Polkas, Valses, Mazourkas and other Circle Dances. Quadrille and Scotch Steps explained so simply that a child may understand them. Dances for Evening Parties. Scotch Reels, Trebles, Grand Marches, Highland Fling and Reel Steps for Ladies and Gentlemen. Irish Jig, Sword Dance, Sean Trubhais etc.

Mr Anderson was aware of the history of dance but gave it short shrift. 'Dancing is, as we know, of a very great antiquity although it was originally practised by the ancients without any regard for method.'

For those who may have had any doubts about the benefits of his lessons he quoted Dr Crichton-Brown who gave a lecture in Birmingham on the subject:

Dancing, if taught at the proper time – that is, very early in life, may discipline large groups into harmonious action, enlarge the dominion of the will, abolish unseemly muscular tricks and antics, develop the sense of equilibrium and impart grace and self-confidence.

Correct etiquette was crucial in the ballrooms at this time. Mr Anderson was ready to advise on this too:

> Gentlemen on entering the Ball-room, and after every dance, lead their partners to a seat by the right arm, bow and retire. Ladies are to sit with hands clasped; gentlemen with hands on knees.

Dance cards were essential and every lady had a card on which was printed the programme of dances for the evening. Mr Anderson spelled out the procedure:

> When any lady or gentleman makes an engagement for a dance, he or she ought to note the name *at once* in the programme in case the engagement be forgotten and another arranged.

Once booked, the gentlemen must follow a formal procedure:

> Gentlemen, before engaging a partner for any dance, should bow and present the right arm, lead the partner to her place in the dance and never leave the dance on any pretence whatever before it is finished.

Gentlemen should:

> change partners often during the evening in order that every lady will enjoy the dance . . . When requiring to use a handkerchief, put it in your pocket immediately when finished with it . . . Avoid all vulgar practices such as biting your nails, making a noise with the feet etc.

The rules applied just as strictly to the ladies:

> No lady, in politeness, can refuse to dance with a gentleman unless she has a previous engagement or feels indisposed. A gentleman so refused may ask the favour of a future dance. Should a gentleman be refused a dance, and afterwards see the lady dancing with another gentleman, he should not *show* his indignation nor appear to notice the action at all.

On the matter of partners the rules were quite clear:

> At a public assembly a gentleman should always if possible be accompanied by a lady . . . Ladies should never dance together if there are disengaged gentlemen in the room and it is highly improper for two gentlemen to do so whilst there are ladies present willing to dance.

Finally, Mr Anderson felt the need to provide 'Hints on Dress': 'Gentlemen should wear a black suit with open vest to show a nice clean shirt front and white or straw-coloured gloves to match . . .' Young ladies were advised to wear 'some light and bright fabric such as tulle, muslin, fine lace etc trimmed with flowers or ribbons, the ribbons generally of a richer colour than the dress.' Gloves should be 'always of the most delicate tint -white, straw, pink or similar and in harmony with the dress of the wearer.'

'Coloured shoes are decidedly vulgar; white and black satin, bronze and black kid are generally fashionable and becoming.' There is a kindly intentioned word for those ladies who suffered from large feet: 'Wear dark stockings and high heels to minimise the effect'. Skirts were to be short to avoid causing the gentlemen to tread on them and head-dresses might be 'of a colour which matches best'.

The final words on dress were reserved for 'Elderly ladies' who were counselled to wear 'silks or satins or dresses of any dark material with a moderate amount of jewellery'.[2]

Mr James Neill (known as Dancie Neill), the well-known dancing teacher of Forfar from 1855 to 1918, had the honour of teaching the Queen Mother when she was a young girl in Glamis Castle. He also instructed three generations of the Atholl family at Blair Castle. His territory covered Alford, Dingwall and Inverness and he cycled or walked the many miles to give his classes. His normal dress was a black jacket, black striped trousers and patent leather shoes, but when teaching at Blair Castle, he always wore the kilt.

Another well-known teacher in the Angus area was Mr John Reid (Dancie Reid), 1890–1942.[3] In his classes deportment and etiquette were emphasised and each class began with a march round the room in time to the music. Mr Reid provided his own music and often demonstrated a step while playing his violin. Girls and boys sat at opposite sides of the room. After some practice steps he selected partners by arranging the children in order of size and matching the tallest boy to the tallest girl and so on down the line. His son William was also a dancing teacher.

Alexander Adamson and his son William were based in Kingskettle and covered the East Neuk of Fife. Adamson was a former pupil of Andrew Doag (1879–1927) who taught in the Cowdenbeath and Lochgelly area. His son William boasted that he had held dancing classes in over 72 different places. He travelled to his classes by bicycle at first, later by motor cycle and latterly by car.

The pattern of classes was much the same everywhere. A class was held each week for fourteen weeks, always on the same night. This allowed the teacher to teach elsewhere on the other four nights of the week. Each night would be divided into two sessions:

6 pm – 7.45 pm juveniles (5 – 14)
8 pm – 10 pm adults

Fees for twelve classes were six shillings. The final class was usually a Ball open to parents and friends, and would cost an extra two shillings and sixpence. As this might prove too expensive for large families, some teachers made a special offer: the first three of a family paid fees and the rest were free. Often a half-time Ball held mid-way through the course would help to encourage the dancers. A successful teacher might have as many as 100 pupils per night, providing a lucrative if somewhat energetic way of earning a living.[4]

When their own ballrooms were not accessible the teachers had to hire halls or use barns or granaries or whatever was available locally. To make dancing possible in such make-shift surroundings they spread powder or candle wax on the floors. It was said that in one hall in the Dumfries area the dancers always finished up covered with a fine white powder as the vigour of their dancing disturbed the flour settled between the floorboards.

Mr Anderson's methods were strict:

> He always started with the Polka, teaching the one, two, three, hop steps first from side to side and then with a turn. Once basic steps were mastered pupils were arranged in couples. Any shyness was counteracted by giving everyone a number so that partners could be summoned to the floor by calling out the numbers. When not on the dancing floor girls had to sit with hands clasped on laps, right hand on top of left. Boys had to sit with hands on knees and legs might not be crossed.[5]

Boys were taught to bow with heels together in front of a partner and say, 'May I have the pleasure of this dance?' Girls were not expected to refuse and were required to curtsey at the end of the dance while the boy would bow.

Dress was important. Most of the men wore their best suits at the Ball while the ladies mostly wore white dresses with flower corsages. Men wore patent leather dancing shoes and often bought the light, moderately high-heeled shoes

The Marine Gardens, Portobello. This shows the extent of a leisure complex which was amongst the first of its kind and would not look out of place today

worn by their partners. Balls for juveniles were from 6 pm to 9 pm followed by the adult Ball from 9 pm to 3 am. All credit goes to the stamina of Mr Anderson, who remained the central figure all evening, leading off the *Grand March* and playing the fiddle.

Music was generally provided by the violin or the piano played by the teacher. At the Balls one or two musicians would be hired to augment the sound. The gramophone and 78 rpm record, invented in 1889, was gradually recognised as a cheap substitute for a band.

As the century progressed and railways made transport easier, the public began to travel more and take advantage of that great British institution, the seaside holiday. Holiday resorts grew and flourished, and the first of the great Palais de Danse ballrooms were built in the new resorts. In Blackpool, the leader in the dance business, there were the three large ballrooms: the huge Empress which could accommodate 3,000 dancers, the Tower and the Palace. Douglas (Isle of Man), Morecambe, Great Yarmouth and Margate all had their Palais. Teachers were employed every year during the season to act as MCs, to popularise new dances and to monitor the behaviour of the dancers.

In Scotland there was the seaside resort of Portobello on the east coast near Edinburgh. Financed by businessman Mr Graham-Yool, the Marine Gardens, billed as 'Scotland's Pleasance by the Sea', was opened on Monday 31 May 1909. In what was an early version of a modern leisure centre, it boasted a roller-skating rink, a band court, promenade hall and a concert pavilion all set in 27 acres of ornamental gardens on the shores of the Firth of Forth.

The Lord Provost of Edinburgh, The Right Honourable James P Gibson MP, braved heavy rain to open the complex and enjoy the music of Herr Meny's White Viennese Band. The ballroom which opened in 1910 was a phenomenal size (97 by 26 yards – half a football pitch). There was seating for 3,000, mainly on settees placed round the ballroom floor. Tables behind the settees held tea or soft drinks but they could be moved to the centre of the floor for Sunday afternoon concert/teas. No alcohol was ever served there. As an opening offer, the first 10,000 patrons could buy a season ticket for seven shillings and sixpence, after which it would cost ten shillings. Daily entrance cost sixpence initially, but rose to a shilling including tea.

To begin with the Waltz was the most popular dance, but Charlie Wood, an Edinburgh dance teacher, was responding to local requirements when he taught Old Time dancing in the ballroom. Old Time (sometimes called Olde Tyme) was the name given to dances in which all dancers on the floor performed the same steps at the same time. This was, perhaps, the only true 'social dancing', as it was essentially a communal pursuit in which partners mixed freely and young and old could perform the steps equally well. The dance historian Franks says:

> all other kinds [of dancing] when one has acquired any marked skill, are to a large extent anti-social, for the tendency is to dance with only one partner and to exclude all others from your own world of movement.[6]

Certainly, the name 'Old Time' alone was enough to put off young 'modern' dancers. The style and the music remained fixed and were soon perceived by the young to be completely out-of-date. The standard teaching of a formal, artificial technique with five positions for the feet and 'pretty movements' was difficult for some pupils to master and impossible for others.

When teaching Old Time, Charlie Wood, who also taught at the Palace Ballroom in Leith, always wore tails and white gloves and to control the dancers he used a baton and a whistle.

Sequence dances were part of the Old Time programme and were dances where a sequence of steps was repeated, usually over sixteen bars. The Veleta and the Military Two-Step (the brain-child of James Finnegan of Manchester) are the main survivors of this period.

This decade began to see the formal recognition of ballroom dancing on a larger scale. In 1909 the first World Ballroom Dancing Championship was held in Paris at the Theatre Sarah Bernhardt. It is possible that this was the first ever big ballroom dancing competition.

The seaside resorts in Britain, with no restrictions on space, were able to build huge ballrooms. Blackpool was now a massive seaside resort which attracted huge numbers of holidaymakers who could take advantage of the new railway system to travel to the coast. Blackpool Tower opened on Whit Monday, 14 May 1894, and the Tower ballroom was in operation shortly after that. The Winter Gardens followed with the ballroom there opening in 1897.

In Glasgow, one enormous hall, then called the Dennistoun Stadium, was destined to play a major role in the dancing city. In 1904, however, it drew the crowds for a different reason. In the stadium that year Buffalo Bill, the buckskinned Colonel William Cody, thrilled the crowds with his Wild West Show, a dramatic rodeo which had a cast of 240 people including 90 Indians and the famous Annie Oakley. There were 200 horses, 200 tons of equipment, covered wagons, a herd of buffalo and the Deadwood stagecoach.

In Britain, dance teachers began to form more associations. In 1903, the UK Alliance of Teachers of Dancing was established; in 1904, the Imperial Society of Dance Teachers; and in 1907, the National Association of Teachers of Dancing.

1910 brought a publishing landmark when the *Dancing Times* was published for the first time as an illustrated monthly magazine. Founded in 1894, it had closed for a year in 1909.

Into this safe, almost dull society there came rumbles of change. The younger generation were chafing and rebelling under the strict rules of the dance. They longed for a free and easy style with more natural movements.

A new dance was introduced from America in 1903 at the KDS (Keen Dancers Society) dances in London. It was called the Boston and although it raised a few eyebrows, at first it failed to catch on. The steps of the dance were similar to the Waltz but the style and shape were quite different. The dance was rectilinear and partners danced right hip to right hip with the man's feet outside his partner's.

The rhythm was different: three even steps taking two bars of music instead of the long, short, short of the Waltz over one bar. This was therefore a slower travelling dance, requiring more space than was generally available on the average ballroom floor. Most importantly, the Boston was the first dance to call for a natural walking movement.

On the whole, the press supported the old rotary Waltz and laughed at the dramatic rectilinear Boston, but it gradually gained support from the younger dancers. It allowed dancers to interpret the music and express themselves through dance. It was also the harbinger of the 'English style' which was to influence dancing for decades to come.

At this time there were three main types of public dance: Academy ballrooms; subscription dances in large hotels; and, increasingly, dance clubs where the best dancers could be found and where well-known bands played up-to-date music.

Up till 1910 dancing was still largely seasonal but by the end of the first decade dancing had become a year-round pursuit. The First World War was only four years away and major events were to lead to major changes in the ballroom.

CHAPTER FOUR

Flappers and Fox Trots

∽ ∾

1910 to 1920

The period between 1910 and 1920 was a time of profound social upheaval which was reflected in dancing styles. By 1910 dancing was accepted as a year-round pastime. It was a social skill required of everyone irrespective of social status. Age was no barrier and whole families would go to a dance together. The Waltz was still top favourite, often featuring in as many as 18 out of the average 24 dances in an evening programme. There was one major difference which was to become more obvious as the decade progressed. Pre-1910 the attraction of dancing was in the actual steps. Post-1910 the attraction was the rhythm.

The popularity of dancing brought demands for more public halls and ball-rooms. The first truly popular English Palais de Danse in London opened in Hammersmith in 1919 offering cheaper dancing than the exclusive West End hotel rates. (At this time Mr C L Heimann founded the Mecca organisation which was to expand into an empire.) Outside London the seaside resorts continued to open much larger premises than in the city of London. In Scotland the newly opened Marine Gardens in Portobello was doing well as an early Palais-style ballroom of massive proportions.

This was the beginning of dance as a growth industry. Adverts in the Glasgow *Evening News* under the heading of 'Tuition' list halls across the city from Springburn to Langside, Bridgeton to Partick, each one attracting local dancers. In Edinburgh too, small halls across the city advertised dancing, some operating on a regular daily basis and others, depending on size, opening on occasions to accommodate functions. One hall in Edinburgh in East Crosscauseway was so small that it was nicknamed 'the Puggienut'. Dancers remember it fondly because the owners would allow regular dancers who could not afford the entrance money to pay the following week – dancing 'on tick'.

In the atmosphere of frantic gaiety that dominated the pre-war period, fancy dress balls were popular and there was a demand for novelty. The slow Waltz, the Lancers, Barn Dance, Cotillon and Polka were beginning to bore the young,

Mr and Mrs J Warren dancing in style

although in Glasgow John and Annie Warren were packing their Albert Halls with dancers who enjoyed sequence dancing. (Before the Warrens took over, the Albert Halls had housed the Racquet Club – where a kind of indoor tennis was played – and they had named their ballroom after Prince Albert.)

From the very beginning, dancing dominated the lives of the Warren family. The four children, Alex, John, Ann and Jessie grew up in an atmosphere dedicated to sequence dancing. In these early days the Warrens advertised: 'Gentlemen one shilling, Ladies, invited'.

By 1912 the Boston form of the Waltz was danced mainly in clubs, with variations like the Judy Walk, Grizzly Bear, Bunny Hug and Turkey Trot. The Turkey Trot, a one-step Rag, consisted of a simple walk as soft and smooth as possible, taking a step to every count of the music, hence the name 'one-step'.

The Bunny Hug had achieved some notoriety in America where it was banned in some dance halls as 'indecent' and a few girls there even took to wearing 'bumpers', prongs that kept their partners at a distance, in an attempt to beat the ban. Young dancers enjoyed experimenting with the Boston in its various forms, but crowded floors killed it as it needed too much space.

A new craze hit the headlines with the introduction of the Argentinian Tango

Determined young dancers would try anything to defeat the ban on the Bunny Hug,
and what was seen by their elders as a hold that was too close

which emerged from Buenos Aires via France. First introduced in 1911, it had an immediate appeal with a new rhythm and an amazing variety of steps. The steps were so numerous that no two teachers taught them in the same way. The dance gained such popularity that a 40,000 word book was written by Gladys Beattie Crocier called *The Tango and How to Dance It*. There were Tango Teas in hotels and restaurants and professional dancers gave exhibition dances all over the country. Jack Diamond of Glasgow's Dancing Academy brought the Tango to the city of Glasgow in 1913 where, along with Mr D G MacNaughton and partners, he demonstrated it in the McLellan Galleries giving rise to a half-column report in the *Glasgow Herald*.

The essential movements of the Tango were a rhythmic, smooth walk, a glide and a sway. Incidentally, the Hesitation Waltz developed out of a combination of the Waltz and the Tango.

At this stage, people began to talk about 'the Jazz', by which they meant syncopated rag-time music which included the One-step, the Tango and the Boston in all their various forms. Jazz was described as 'strict rhythm without melody' although A H Franks said that 'jazz has nothing to do with rhythm and syncopation. Jazz refers to the instruments on which the music is played . . . also an important element is extemporisation'.[1] He suggested that the word Jazz may have come from the French word *'jaser'* which means 'to gossip' as it perfectly describes the 'gossip' between instruments.

In 1912 Irving Berlin wrote his famous 'Alexander's Ragtime Band'. Rag-Time was born. Described as Negro rhythm combined with evangelistic hymn tunes, this syncopated One-Step captured the mood of the moment. Rust describes it as 'music with 2, 4 or 6 beats to the bar, but while the duration of the bar remains constant, the rhythm becomes irregular, jumping here, hesitating there and constantly displacing the normal beat'.[2]

Herr Gottlieb's Orchestra recorded Berlin's music on 78 rpm records and it became a smash hit with the younger set. For the first time a split appeared between dancing generations instead of the previous class split. At first it was not a complete division because families still danced together, but the older generation tended to adhere to the older dances and were not attracted by the wild rhythms coming from America, while the younger set revelled in the freedom of the newer dances.

The 1914–18 War had an immediate effect on dancing. In Portobello, the Marine Gardens ballroom area was closed to dancers for a while and used by the 5th Royal Scots as its main sleeping quarters. As the War broke out in the holiday month of August, most dance schools were closed anyway. However, by the time it came to September and the beginning of the season, it had been decided to continue to dance as a morale booster for the troops and their families. The change in the style of dancing reflected the faster pace of life and the more frantic style of troops on leave determined to enjoy themselves.

There was the energetic Maxixe which enjoyed a brief popularity in early 1914. This combined a Polka movement with a Cuban *habanera* rhythm and added

African syncopation for good measure. It was not destined to last, although its influence was to be seen much later in the Samba.

In 1914 a more important new dance was on the way across the Atlantic. It was a development from a series of dances starting with the Boston. This dance, which was to become the most popular ballroom dance of all time, was the Fox Trot. Where Ragtime was a One-Step in which dancers were required to walk smoothly across the floor taking one step to every count of the music, this new dance, the Fox Trot, added rhythm and trotting movements.

The early basic movement started with a walk for four steps (2 bars) followed by a run of seven quick steps bringing the right foot to the back of the left on the eighth bar. An early, rollicking version of the dance had been seen in the American Ziegfeld Follies where Harry Fox performed trotting steps in the dance position to 4/4 music.

A US dance teacher, Mr Oscar Duryea, demonstrated and taught the dance to members of the Imperial Society of Teachers of Dancing in London in 1914. However, Mr D G MacLennan, the Edinburgh dance teacher, had seen it during a lecture tour in America and wasted no time in introducing and promoting it directly to Scottish dancers. In no time this new dance had ousted all competition.

Of all the dances in the ballrooms, the Fox Trot seemed best suited to the times. The trotting movements and ragtime rhythm were new and different. Young men on leave from the War wanted to dance but had no time for formal instruction. Parents and girlfriends wanted to spend free time with them without the discipline of dancing lessons. The Fox Trot with its lack of formal steps was easy for everyone to pick up and they came along in droves to the ballrooms.

There were inevitable variations. A new tune in 1916, 'Underneath the Stars', gave rise to a smoother Fox Trot which the *Dancing Times* christened The Saunter.

It was not only the style of dancing that was changing. The music was changing too. In late 1917 the Americans arrived bringing the latest Jazz music from America. This new music needed new instruments. The strings which had long been the mainstay of the orchestras were replaced by banjos, saxophones and trap drums. Orchestras were renamed Jazz Bands. Eventually even the sousaphones and banjos were superseded by bass and guitars. Many of the old bands found the new music impossible to play and there was an upsurge of new Ragtime bands. Another effect of the War was that the once popular Austrian and German bands were out of favour and had to be replaced.

Throughout all of this period dance floors were crowded with dancers day and night, especially in Glasgow. After the 1914–18 War was over, a new figure destined to play a large part in the dance band scene arrived back in Scotland. His name was Louis Freeman. Louis, who had won the Bechstein Gold Medal for piano playing in Glasgow in 1912, went to America in 1914 where he played in the Palace Theatre for famous names like Al Jolson, Sophie Tucker and Eddie Cantor. Unable to join up because of a heart murmur, Louis returned to Glasgow where he played jazz in the Carlton in St Vincent Street. Louis discovered that there was a need for dance bands on the transatlantic steamers that left Glasgow for America on a regular basis. At that time the *Caledonian*, the *California* and the *Transylvania* ran from Yorkhill Quay in Glasgow to New York taking five days each way. Two others ran from Ayr to Montreal. Louis set up an agency to supply bands to these ships and was given the contract to supply all the music on the boats. The musicians came to be known as Louis Freeman's Navy. Billy MacGregor, who was a drummer on the steamers, recalled that the positions were very much coveted. The pay was good and there were not many opportunities for spending, so the bandsmen could be well off by the time they reached home shores again.

The craze for dancing continued to grow. It followed the pattern of dance mania that seemed always to come in the wake of war. Cecil Sharp and A P Oppe noted a rise in demand for dance teachers following the end of the Napoleonic Wars; after the French Revolution in 1800 dancing salons opened in Paris; and there was another popular craze in the aftermath of the American Civil War. Possibly the mass feeling of relief at the advent of peace is best expressed through dance.[3] The end of the War in 1918 brought an influx of young American soldiers from France on their way to be demobbed. They brought with them fresh styles and movements.

Tea-dancing was very fashionable. Every afternoon dancers would arrive at five with a partner. The ladies wore hats pulled down over their noses and skirts trimmed with heavy silk fringes. Afternoon tea was served at tables set round the floor, and the patrons could dance or listen to a band.

In January 1920 the Edinburgh *Evening News* reported:

> Apparently the young people of today are not satisfied with dancing almost every night of the week and therefore the 'Dance Tea' has been introduced where they can jazz to their heart's content all afternoon as well.
>
> This form of amusement has become increasingly popular and at these functions many very pretty afternoon frocks are to be seen.[4]

Afternoon frocks were not on the agenda of an important meeting in the Prince's Galleries, London, in 1920, where 300 worried dance teachers from all over the UK had gathered to discuss a serious problem. In a nutshell, if there were no set steps it would be impossible to teach dancing. The free-style Fox Trot and syncopated jazz music represented a real threat to the profession. Alex Warren, who had travelled from Glasgow to attend the meeting, said, 'As a matter of urgency it was agreed that the teachers should try to stamp out freak steps in the ballroom.' There was general disapproval of exaggerated dips, steps where both feet were off the ground and side steps (as in the Shimmy) which impeded other dancers. A sub-committee decided on the basic steps of the Fox Trot.

By standardising the dances the teachers were, of course, protecting their own

The early elegance of The Albert in Glasgow

interests, but they were also opening up the possibility of competition, which was to play an important part in the further spread of ballroom dancing. Another by-product of accepted standardisation of dances was the emergence of dancing professionals. The dancing scene was set for more change.

While the general trend was towards change, there was still some disagreement about the style of dancing within the various ballrooms. On 1 January 1920 an advert in the Edinburgh *Evening News* gives a clear picture of the stance of the old guard:

> Stewart's Academy, Abbeymount – 2 halls, 3 orchestras, the largest, most up-to-date ballroom in the city. No jazzing or vulgar dancing allowed. Anyone not complying with the rules of the ballroom will be ejected and no money returned.[5]

On the other hand, in the same year there was an notice for 'Edinburgh's Palais de Danse – The Wemyss Ballroom.' It advertised:

> The Jazz maniac's Jazz Band with Symon Stungo on piano, Nicholas Ivanoff on violin and banjoline and Freddy James on Trap Drums. Everyone will Shimmy now. Opening night Wed. 8th September. Admission Ladies, two shillings, Gents two and six-pence.The ballroom that made jazzing fashionable.[6]

(The Shimmy was a dance in which the knees and toes were turned in followed by the 'frisson' or shake of the bottom, considered by some to be vulgar and shameless).

46

In Glasgow in 1917 the Albert remained faithful to the older dances. The programme for the annual ball consisted of: the Carina, La Rose Waltz, Pas de Quatre, Twinkle Trot, La Mascotte, Amelia Waltz, Mayfair One-Step, Boston Two-Step Maxima, Jutland and Reels, Quadrilles and Waltzes.

Adverts in the Glasgow *Evening News* at this time show that the Albert was not alone. Quadrille Assemblies, as many as eight in an evening, were still attracting dancers throughout this decade. There were signs of the influence of the young Alex Warren in 1920 when the Albert advertised the Niagara One-Step and the Pussyfoot Glide.

The end of this decade saw the arrival of new ballrooms in Edinburgh. It also saw a significant change in the advertising policy of the Edinburgh *Evening News* which passed without comment. Until early September 1920, Assemblies and Ballrooms had always appeared under the heading 'Tuition'. From 8 December 1920 the adverts appeared under a new heading – 'Dancing'. It seems that it was no longer necessary to disguise the activity under the cloak of 'education'.

The *Evening News* of Saturday 4 December 1920 announced the opening of Edinburgh's newest and largest ballroom, the Grafton Assembly Rooms at West Tollcross. The owner, Mr P A Ogg, planned a Charity Opening on Tuesday 7 December at which double tickets would be 25 shillings and single tickets 15 shillings.[7]

December also saw adverts for Mrs Cameron Walker's Superior Assembly in the York Hall, Picardy Place; Vall's dancing on Portobello Promenade; dancing at the Crown Ballroom in Lothian Street, and advance notice of the opening of the Leith Central ballroom (late Queen's Hotel) on 1 January 1921.

The most significant newcomer was the Palais de Dance at Fountainbridge which opened on a Friday – Christmas Eve 1920. The money taken on the opening night amounted to £170 and the whole amount was donated to the Edinburgh Royal Infirmary. January 1921 saw separate advertisements for the Fountainbridge Palais in the Edinburgh *Evening News*, making the point that this was to set new standards of dancing for Edinburgh. It boasted: 'Daily sessions: 3pm – two and sixpence; 7.30pm – three and sixpence; 2,000 can dance at one time. Two celebrated dance bands.'

The following March it was offering: 'A buffet lounge, tea rooms, dancing partners, bewildering surprises, wonderful new musical dance selections, brilliant flashlight illuminations, gorgeous decorations and fantastic stunts.'

By the end of 1920 there were warring styles of dancing, each representing a totally different image. There was the highly dramatic image of the Tango which was epitomised by the cinema idol, Rudolph Valentino; the crazy jazz style of the young flappers; and the elegant, light, agile style of the Foxtrot of Jack Buchanan or Fred Astaire. This confusion of dance styles left many competent, old-fashioned waltzers lost and feeling out of touch. Many older men did not feel able to make the effort to change to a more active, demanding dance. The result was that many young wives needed partners, preferably young partners who could dance well. The customers demanded and the market was poised to provide.

CHAPTER FIVE

Rise of the Big Palais
Ballrooms

എ ൜

1920 to 1930

In the dazzling twenties of the 'flappers' and 'bright young things' and despite (or perhaps, because of) the vicious post-war recession, the country was gripped by dancing fever. Dancing enjoyed a post-war boom on a grand scale and nowhere more so than in Glasgow. Glasgow was dancing mad.

During this period, huge 'Palais' ballrooms sprang up inviting patrons into a world of plush splendour, glittering lights and syncopated rhythms. There were eleven major ballrooms in Glasgow, more per head of population than anywhere else in the country. Edinburgh had five, and London, with its chronic lack of space, could boast only three or four. There were also hundreds of smaller but nonetheless popular ballrooms in the cities and towns scattered throughout the country.

Dancing represented an escape from the extremes of real poverty or the ennui of leisure and wealth. With Income Tax at sixpence in the pound (2.5%), those with money could afford to spend lavishly. For some, it was important to learn to dance because dancing could be a passport from the dole queue to the glamour and prestige of work in the ballrooms.

The most coveted positions, attracting substantial salaries, belonged to the dancing professionals employed to demonstrate new steps on the dance floors. The top professionals became stars earning admiration as exhibition dancers.

At another level, ballroom managements hired dancers to partner patrons, sometimes providing the female employees with dresses and usually paying them by the dance. Young, unemployed men would practice dance steps with their partners on street corners before venturing into the ballrooms in the steadfast hope of being 'discovered' and invited to join the elite staff. With so many eager to learn, dance schools continued to flourish, and newspapers, aware of the craze, would publish supplements detailing the steps of the latest dances.

Ballrooms vied with one another to offer the best facilities. Top dance couples from all over the country were engaged to give special exhibitions; novelty evenings added spice to the programmes; and competitions offered fabulous prizes.

This was the era of dancing superstars. One of the most famous couples, Santos Casani and his partner Jose Lennard, eventually came to be immortalised on film, dancing on the roof of a London taxi. They were adored by their fans and were paid enormous fees for appearing in ballrooms around the country. It was recorded that when they taught at the Glasgow Norwood Ballroom for a week they were paid £100 a *day*. (This at a time when a working man might earn £2 a week.)

The standardisation of dances emerged after three informal conferences of dance teachers from all over Britain. The committee formed from these conferences included Victor Sylvester, Josephine Bradley, Eve Tynegate-Smith, Muriel Simmonds and Mrs Lisle Humphries (later Lady Peacock). They deliberated during 1920 and 1921 and set minimum standards for the basic figures of the Fox Trot, Waltz and Tango. The Waltz was eventually set in the pattern of step, step and feet together which was a further progress towards the English Style.

In fact, style was an important element which the teachers wanted to control. They recommended that in modern dancing the knees should be kept together in passing and the feet parallel. They also urged that all eccentric steps be abolished and that dancers should do their best always to progress round the room.

Competitions had started in Paris but now they began in Britain. The first major event for dancers was held in Blackpool at the Blackpool Festival during Easter week, 1920. Events were limited to three competitions to discover three new sequence dances in Waltz, Two-Step and Fox Trot time.

There was no audience and competitors displayed their dances in front of a panel of adjudicators during the day. At 4 pm, entrants were summoned to the ballroom where the winners of the day were announced. In the evening, the first, second and third winners demonstrated and taught their new dances to the general public at an evening ball.

On the final night, all first-prize-winners competed in public for the 'Sharples Challenge Shield'. One of the adjudicators from the *Dancing Times* was Mr P J S Richardson. He recorded that this was the start of the North of England Championships which, at this time, included Scotland.

The competition took place again in 1921 and this time one of the winners was Charles Wood from Edinburgh with a dance called 'Très Chic'. Amongst the audience was Alex Warren with his mother, Annie, and sister, Jessie. They could not have known that this was the beginning of a series of events that would shake the safe world of sequence dancing at the Albert.

In 1922, for the first time, London hosted the World Championships, when the Waltz section was won by Victor Sylvester and his partner, Miss Phyllis

Clarke. The four championship dances were the Waltz, Fox Trot, One Step and Tango and there were three categories: amateur, professional and mixed.

That same year, the *Dancing Times* Conference studied the Tango and agreed to use only modern tunes for the dance and adhere to a tempo of 30 bars to the minute.

At Blackpool, stage and Morris dancing were added to the programme and there was a special display of Scottish Dancing by Messrs McConnachie, Charles Wood, George Dixon and S N Morgan.

1922 was to be a pivotal year for the Warrens. Alex and Jessie Warren came second to the great Adela Roscoe and her husband, H A Clifton, who won the Sharples Shield with the Royal Empress Tango. Alex also met and married Nellie Lees, a floormistress in the Winter Gardens.

As an extra stroke of luck, Adela Roscoe had other commitments and Alex and Jessie were invited to stay in Blackpool for three months to demonstrate dances including the Royal Empress Tango.In the middle of all this glory, Jessie, the darling of the family with a brilliant dancing future, caught an infection and died on 28 March 1923 at the age of 18.

Alex and his family were devastated. His mother, Annie Warren never danced again. It may also have brought to a head a disagreement between Alex and his father.

For some time, Alex had been trying to persuade John Warren that he should modernise the Albert and change the style of dancing he taught. Young Alex Warren had served his apprenticeship teaching children's classes from the age of 15. The most favoured dances then were the Veleta, the Amelia Waltz and Quadrilles and Lancers. Now he wanted the Albert to take on the newer dances. The feud deepened with the arrival of the Charleston in 1923. John refused to see the impact of the new dance. Alex, at the age of 20, left home and moved to Blackpool where he was appointed floor manager – the youngest dancing chief in Britain.

The feud lasted for almost two years, but by 1925, John Warren was forced to admit that Alex had been right. He tempted Alex back to Glasgow with glittering plans for expansion and an honest admission that he had been wrong. As his son had forecast, the Charleston had taken over Glasgow. There had never been anything like it. Alex recalled that you could go through Glasgow and see people practising the steps at bus stops or in shop queues. Nobody stood still when the Charleston was the rage.

Alex returned home and set the Albert on course to be the leading ballroom in Scotland. His brother John and sister Anne were exhibition dancers and John eventually married his dancing partner, Miss Dorothy Dawn (née Persichini).

Without doubt, the hit of that decade was the Charleston. 'This was originally a Negro round dance which was discovered in 1923 among Negro dock workers in Charleston, North Carolina. In October 1923 the Ziegfeld Follies introduced it at the New Amsterdam Theatre and afterwards it became part of a show "Runnin' Wild" which toured the States.'[1]

Robert Sielle and Annette Mills, the couple who first demonstrated the Charleston.
Annette Mills achieved lasting fame as the manipulator of Muffin the Mule on
Children's Television

The Charleston combined winging and lifting steps with the Fox Trot walk and the Two-Step. The dance quickly became the rage in America and it was introduced to Britain at a tea-dance in London at Ciro's Club, arranged by the *Dancing Times* for dancing teachers. The couple who first demonstrated the Charleston that day were Annette Mills (sister of the actor John Mills) and her partner, Robert Sielle. They had returned from a visit to the States and were soon touring the country giving demonstrations of the new dance.

The Charleston was a violent dance which was condemned by many as freakish, degenerate and vulgar. Doctors warned of permanent distortion of the ankles or even shocks to the body leading to paralysis. Ballroom managements were more concerned about physical damage to other dancers on the floor. Notices appeared on ballroom walls – P C Q – Please Charleston Quietly!

Victor Sylvester described the dance and its effects:

> It was an immediate hit, and, when the Prince of Wales took lessons from a girl called Beryl Evetts, who had won the first Star Championship and afterwards taught at the Café de Paris, nothing could stop it. Wherever you went people seemed to be practising the Charleston – in bus queues, in Tube stations waiting for a train, at street corners, in shops; even policemen on point duty were seen doing the steps – because in practically every ballroom in London every second dance was the Charleston, although ministers fulminated against it from their pulpits, schools banned it, and various cultural societies staged protest marches . . . personally I don't think there has ever been anything quite like it.[2]

The disadvantage of the dance was that people were continually getting their legs bruised and thousands of women's stockings were laddered. After some time the dance was modified by the Imperial Society to a more graceful version called the Flat Charleston, a version in which the feet never left the floor, and the dance was ultimately incorporated into the Quick Step. The compulsive rhythm was enough to ensure its survival as one of the greats.

Another product of a Broadway hit was the Black Bottom. This was a dance of stamps, knee sways and shuffle steps described by Curt Sachs as 'a lively mixture of side-turns, stamps, skating-glides, skips and leaps.'[3] If anything, the establishment was even more outraged by this one.

In 1924 the Ballroom Branch of the Imperial Society of Teachers of Dancing was founded. This was an important move. The Society journal published a syllabus of examination for admission to the Society and this was the foundation for what became known as 'The English Style' which was also adopted by Scottish members. The basic requirements were: knowledge of dance music, knowledge of dance steps, and good style and carriage.

By 1925, the One-Step had been replaced by the Quick Foxtrot which eventually became the Quickstep in 1929, thus completing the standard set of dances: Waltz, Fox Trot, Tango and Quickstep.

Also in 1925, there was the first of the famous 'Star' competitions to be held by the *Star* newspaper annually for the next seven years. Although this was a major event for dancers, it was never in the same category as the Blackpool Festival. This was partly because competition in Blackpool was open to all comers and it could therefore truly claim to be a 'world' championship whereas the Star competitors were selected from those dancers considered best in each area.

1929 saw the formation of the Official Board of Ballroom Dancing at the *Dancing Times* conference. Dance teachers were generally happy about the new standards and the various upholding bodies but there was a price to pay. Dancers were tending to divide into 'competition' dancers on the one hand and 'social' or 'crush' dancers on the other. The former were keen to improve their dancing techniques while the latter simply wanted to dance in the company of friends. Either way, there was no doubt about the popularity of dancing in the twenties.

Farquhar MacRae, a lifelong dancer, recalled how it was in Glasgow at this time:

> I first danced in 1922 in the City Halls. I'd never had a lesson but I watched for a bit and then I joined in the One-Step to the tune, 'Valencia'. The One-Step was a very good dance to learn because there were no chassées in it, just open dancing, but it was very fast so it was a bit frightening.
>
> Later I went to Diamond's Academy. I remember the Dancing Master there. He was very strict and he tapped your shoulder with his stick if you made a mistake. The favourite dance there was the Mazurka Waltz.
>
> In 1923 I won my first medal for a Fox Trot to the music, 'I'll see you in my Dreams'. I danced in the 'Vicky Rooms' in Victoria Road where there were always great dancers, and in the Marina at Bridgeton Cross. My partner at the time was Lizzie Edgar and we started to compete. We won the slow Fox Trot in the F & F Palais and also in the Dennistoun Palais.
>
> As well as demonstrators, in the twenties many halls had dancing partners. At a kiosk a girl gave out tickets – sixpence a dance. There would be 26 dances every afternoon, one every six minutes, and you could tell the time by looking at the number of the dance. Dancing partners didn't have paper qualifications then so they were just interviewed by the management of the ballroom and taken on the strength of their

Dancers at the Glasgow Locarno in the twenties

appearance and ability to dance. Mostly they were on a one pound retainer and then they were allowed one half of the sixpence fee. Top partners who could compete were in great demand. They were often booked for the whole afternoon [3.00 pm to 5.30 pm] or evening [8.00 pm to 11.00 pm]. That would mean dancing 26 dances in the afternoon and 30 in the evening.

Some of them did have perks. Grateful customers would give the men new shirts or suits, and the girls new shoes or dresses. I knew one dancing partner who got a car for Christmas and another who got a double-fronted shop! With Income Tax at sixpence in the pound, those who were earning had tons of money to spend and could afford to be very generous.

The twenties and thirties were a very dressy age. Ordinary working men would come home from work and press their trousers before tea, Brylcreem their hair and part it in a centre shed. Ladies wore knee-length frocks or formal long dresses. At big competitions dress was always formal and the Plaza always insisted on evening dress. I remember one dress my wife had in the thirties. She had it made by a dressmaker, Mrs Mulholland. Chiffon was a shilling the yard and there were 30 yards in the frock. It cost five guineas. With it she won the prize for the best dress at the Snowball Dance at the Plaza.

A boy always asked a girl to dance, although sometimes he just nodded and put his hand out. In the small halls, boys and girls stood apart between dances, but there was no segregation in the larger halls.

Places were packed. There were at least 70 places where you could dance in Glasgow in the twenties and thirties. This was a dance-crazy era. Dancing was the premier thought in mind. Nobody sat in the hall. They stood at either end waiting for the beat of the drum so they could dive for a favourite partner. There was always a rush across the floor for the partners who were good dancers.

Every hall had its own character. In the 'Vicky Rooms' there were about half a dozen partners you could hire but they just stood like the rest. The Hibs in Garngad was tough. There they danced with their caps on. The St Andrew's Halls was one of the poshest. Some councillors were appalled to see folk walk in wearing their ordinary shoes instead of dancing shoes. Bobby Jones made a big success of that place despite a lot of opposition from neighbouring ballrooms at the start. He took over the Berkeley later and then moved to the Ayr Ballroom where, in the forties, American troops packed the building every night at five shillings a head.

In those days, for two and sixpence you could leave the south side, go east to the Dennistoun Palais by tram, pay admission and cloakroom tickets, buy a cup of tea, cake and biscuit and have something left.

One of the most beautiful ballrooms used to be Henglers Circus and it then became the Waldorf. The Red Barn had a huge coal fire at one end. Green's Playhouse had Charlie Watson (famed for 'If I had You') as a big attraction in the twenties.

Warren's, Diamond's, Walker's and Mackintosh's were all very strict. You would choose your ballroom for the evening by reading the adverts of competitions or big bands. Joe Loss and Roy Fox were my favourites.

Dancing lessons in the twenties cost one guinea for a course of five or five shillings each.

Edinburgh was also enjoying a dance craze. One patron, Tam Morton, remembered:

I first started dancing at the Assembly Rooms in Leith in 1924 shortly after leaving school and starting work. The Assembly Rooms were run by Danny Hanley who played the piano accordion and Rab Scullion was on the drums. We boys were allowed to dance together while learning and it wasn't as easy as it looked – especially trying to turn. Anyway, an older pal who could dance had us practising at the street corner during the week and we soon learned to dance with girls. As the boys lined one side of the ball-room and the girls the other, it meant crossing the hall to pick up your partner.

After a while I graduated to other small halls with three or four piece bands: the Masonic Hall, Charlotte Street: Glendinning's, Pilrig Street, and the Corner Rooms at the foot of Ferry Road. These were mainly Saturday night dances but during the week there was Kinnaird's Hall in the Kirkgate where Hanley played alternate nights with another accordionist, 'Fiery Carrie', who had only one eye. The Corner Rooms had Jack Lawson on piano, 'Sodger' Veitch on sax, Alfie Robertson on drums and there was also a violinist.

The Assembly Rooms in Edinburgh continued to flourish right into the twentieth century. In the Edinburgh *Evening Dispatch* of 1922 the changes were recorded:

> Born 1786 and Still Going Strong
>
> From time to time alterations and improvements have been made to the premises but the ballroom and 'Crush' room are in their original form. Two rooms have now disappeared which used to play an important part of the assemblies. These were known as the East and West servant's waiting rooms and in the days when sedan chairs were used it was here that the bearers awaited their mistresses' pleasure.
>
> Up to the outbreak of War catering was done on the premises but after that it was farmed out to caterers. Music was supplied at the Voucher Balls by Mr J P Ross and his orchestra while Mr James Gilchrist's Band played at Assemblies.

At the same time as the older ballrooms continued to flourish there were also the magnificent new Palais ballrooms which were opening up in both cities. Many of these advertised 'sprung floors'.

The acquisition of sprung floors quickly became the mark of a ballroom where the management took dancing seriously. Social dancers might be happy to dance on any flat surface but keen dancers and professionals demanded a smooth surface with no splinters and with shock-absorbing qualities that would protect them from impact injuries. Mark Foley's book on the subject gives detailed information.

Sprung floor systems were 'area elastic', which meant that their smooth, stable surface 'floated' or flexed on an underlying cushion. There were three traditional types of floor suspension. In the first, actual metal coil springs were mounted on a strong concrete base. Battens were laid across the springs and the whole area was covered with smooth ply sheeting and finished with a tongue and groove wood flooring. The second method simply employed a lattice of timber layers under the ply and wood strip flooring; and the third used rubber pads under timber battens to give resilience.

As dancing was not permitted on Sundays, the ballroom at the Marine Gardens became
a massive tea-room where patrons could listen to concerts of classical music

The surface layer had to be of a dense, close-grained timber such as maple or
beech, finished to the glassy perfection of yellow silk. As a final touch, managements would sprinkle a powder called Slipperene on the floor before dancing
began, and dancers could glide across the floor as if it was a skating rink.

In Edinburgh the already established Marine Gardens was developing into a
major venue which attracted dancers from all over the country – even from
Glasgow with its many ballrooms. Admission was one shilling from 8.00 pm to
11.00 pm. Saturdays cost one and sixpence but this included a free ticket for the
following Wednesday worth threepence.

Sundays were always big concert days. There was no dancing but the hall was
set out with tables for afternoon tea where patrons could enjoy the music of

world famous violinists like De Groot or Albert Sandler. The concerts continued into the evenings and one patron remembered: 'We listened to visiting stars and it was all classy and sedate music. We bought fruit drinks for a shilling and made them last all night.'

In 1923 the financial manager was Mr Fraser. The ballroom was still owned by Mr Graham-Yool who regularly welcomed popular stars like Douglas Fairbanks Junior when they visited the city.

It was customary to 'book' a settee when patrons arrived. Girls could attend with girlfriends or boyfriends and would keep to the same settee all evening. The settees – reputed to number 1,000 – were placed round the ballroom, and prospecting dancers would promenade round the hall in search of a partner.

During the twenties the Marine Gardens, like many other large ballrooms, provided partners who were not hired to teach but were simply to dance with. One lady remembered clearly how she was hired. Elizabeth Raeburn started dancing at the age of 16 and learned in Mavor's Ballroom in Pitt Street, Edinburgh. Mavor's was the place to go in that area, and there she learned the Two-step, One-step, Fox Trot, Tango and Waltz. In the season 1923 to 1924 she

This early photograph shows the manager of the Marine Gardens, Mr Fraser, third from the left, and Mr Graham-Yool, the owner, seventh from the left. The first couple on the right are champions Philp and Scutts who originally came from Edinburgh

was taken on as dancing instructress in Stewart's, Abbeymount. The pay was poor. Dancers were charged threepence a dance and the five instructresses waiting on the small balcony above the band were given one penny per dance. (Stewart's was very strict and was reckoned to be mainly for beginners. Old Mrs Stewart didn't like dancers to come if they could dance already. She was killed in a motor accident and the ballroom was taken over by her sons.)

One night in 1925 Elizabeth's fortunes changed dramatically when she went to dance at the Marine Gardens. Mr Fraser, the manager, recognised her. They had been neighbours in Rose Street when they were children. When he asked what she was doing she told him about her work. He said, 'We're needing another instructress here. There's a dress up in the dressing room. Go up and try it on.'

It was black velvet with a black velvet panel and orange crêpe de chine insets. It fitted me perfectly. He said I would have to dance with one of their instructors to prove I was good enough. We laughed when he called over Jack Telford. I taught him to dance on Portobello Promenade.

I took the dress home and my aunt steamed it, washed the crêpe de chine, ironed it and sewed it in again. The night I started at the Marine Gardens I walked in that door and I felt like a million pounds. There was a roped off circle for the instructors and instructresses – fifteen of each – and the area was always called The Paddock. My seat was waiting for me and I was so excited I felt that it was the greatest thing that ever happened to me.

I was to be paid a basic thirty shillings a week plus twopence for every dance [Marine Gardens charged patrons sixpence a dance].

It was a huge place with anything from 1,000 to 2,000 dancers a night. Each night there were forty four dances and I danced every one of the forty four. The thing was that I was a local and everyone knew me. There was a little room behind the bandstand used by visiting celebrities. I was once allowed to play Banker there in a gambling session with Annette Mills and Robert Sielle between the tea-time session and the evening session. I was only allowed to put sixpence on and Robert Sielle was very kind and helped me to play.

Shoes were a big expense. I needed a new pair every three weeks. The dresses were provided by the ballroom – identical for the 15 girls. I remember one year we had tussore dresses with our initials in red on the pocket. One season we had a floral dress and another time a black one with orchids.

The instructors I remember were Tom McCall (head instructor), Walter Lumsden, Billy Chisholm, Jack Campbell, Jack Telford and Jimmy Briggs. The instructresses were Innes Halliday (head instructress), Greta Scobie, May Wilson, May Bruce, Sadie King, Betty King, Ella Mathieson and Elsie Fergusson.

Elizabeth was married in 1925 but continued to be an instructress until she was expecting her first child. She had met her husband in the Marine Gardens and he occasionally sang with the band – at that time directed by Billy Reid.

More memories of that time come from Tam Morton:

The staff of the Marine Gardens including the manager, Mr Fraser (centre), the band and some of the instructors and instructresses

Around 1925 to 1926 I discovered the Marine Gardens which was huge and palatial-looking to us. It had a full orchestra of ten or twelve pieces and they all wore dinner suits, with the leader in full dress suit. It was called The New Rialto Orchestra, led by Leslie D Jeffries, who looked immaculate in his evening suit with the handkerchief tucked in his collar to rest his violin on. There was Billy Reid who was second pianist and played occasional numbers on the piano accordion, and an Edinburgh lad, Arthur Young, who played saxophone and piano with a special tune he composed. He went on to be a pianist and arranger of the orchestra at the Grand Hotel, Eastbourne, and he broadcast often in the Palm Court Orchestra. Mr Jeffries played a lovely Tango tune called 'Très Jolie' but he eventually fought and lost a law suit over who had written it. There was one tune which the band belted out with the clarinets in full voice. It was called 'Deep Henderson' [Brian Inglis used it as his signature tune many years later in a TV programme called All Our Yesterdays'].

Two young men made a guest appearance at the Marine Gardens dancing the Charleston. Bert and Al Delfont were to become better known in later life as Sir Bernard Delfont (brother of Lew Grade) and Hal Monty, comedian. At that time they earned £15 a week dancing in the ballrooms. Bernie and his partner called the act The Delfont Boys and they decided to keep the name Delfont in preference to their own names, Bernie Winogradsky and Albert Sutan.[5]

(Lew Grade had been named Charleston Champion of the World at a competition in the Albert Hall in 1926. He formed a double act with Al Gold touring theatres as 'Grad and Gold, The Charleston Champions'.)

By the late twenties Great Britain had been divided into 24 districts for the purposes of Amateur Ballroom Championships. There were only two in Scotland, at the Marine Gardens and at the Locarno in Glasgow. Organised by the Columbia Gramophone Company, the event was managed by the famous Santos Casani. Prizes ranged from silver cups to the very latest Portable Grafonolas (early types of gramophones) valued at four pounds fifteen shillings each, and cigarette cases for ladies and gentlemen. Included in the list of judges were Victor and Mrs Sylvester and Jose Lennard, partner to Casani. According to the programme, 3,120 people witnessed the Edinburgh District Final.

The Scottish Championship of the Amateur Ballroom Dancing Company of Great Britain was decided at the Marine Gardens on 14 December 1928, when the winners were Mr A Steel and Miss Macdonald (of Glasgow).

The arrival of the 'Talkies' in 1929 had affected ballroom attendances in the Marine Gardens, but the novelty soon wore off and regulars returned. One manager kept graphs of daily and weekly attendances, and recorded 900 dancers during one week in May 1929 and 1,300 in May 1931.

Resident bands changed over the years. In 1927 there was the Ambassador's Orchestra with Lou Simmonds on violin.

The Marine Gardens now had rivals in the city. The Fountainbridge Palais also had dancing partners but these were eventually replaced by demonstration

Visiting celebrities at the Marine Gardens. Santos Casani is centre, beside Jose Lennard third from the left, partnered by Philp and Scutts

An early photo of Tim Wright's band at the Edinburgh Plaza

couples. The Palais always gave big prizes to dance competition winners. In 1928 prizes were 'fully fitted Lady's and Gentlemen's wardrobes'. The Palais Club had a membership in 1928 of over 500 and it grew fast as dancing became the major pastime.

In October 1921 the Grafton Assembly Rooms were renamed Maxime's. The press reported, 'Mr Thayer (formerly of the Palais) begs to announce that he will open shortly a beautiful new Dancing Salon at Tollcross'.[6] In November, the Grand Opening Ball revealed a Japanese Lounge, French and Turkish rooms and a Winter Garden. Dancers danced to the music of two London bands. Admission was seven and sixpence and evening or dinner dress was mandatory.

Maxime's flourished. There were charity balls, amateur championships and visiting cabaret artistes like Mark Griver, the singing banjoist.

Also in Edinburgh, in September 1926, the Plaza Salon de Danse and café opened its doors. It was built in that year by Mr Charles Jones as an upper story to his new motor showroom. There were two ballrooms, the main one large and the East ballroom smaller and more intimate. The resident band was Lionel Murray's London Dance Band, there was a staff of 20 and dancing partners were provided.

Like all other ballrooms, the Plaza was not licensed for alcohol but patrons had a choice of tea, coffee, Horlicks, cold milk, hot milk or Bovril. High teas cost one and ninepence and wedding guests were catered for at four and sixpence per head. The 'usual wedding menu' for four and sixpence was: tea, coffee, various sandwiches, sandwich fingers, muffins, cakes, cut cake, shortbreads, assorted pastries, biscuits and chocolate biscuits, fruit and wine jellies and creams, trifle, fruit salad, ices handed round later and 'aerated waters'(lemonades).

For grander affairs there was the five and sixpence menu: Soup or grapefruit, choice of hot joints or beefsteak pies with vegetables and potatoes, cold meats and salad, choice of two sweets, tea, coffee, biscuits and cheese, sandwiches, cakes, biscuits and ices served later.

Meanwhile, over in Glasgow, the Albert, under the guidance of Alex Warren, was gaining a reputation as the home of good dancers. There were twelve white-gloved dancing partners in the Albert who earned a basic three pounds a week, although tips were generous ranging from five pound notes to gold cufflinks or even, on occasion, cars. The ballroom charged sixpence a dance or twelve and sixpence a night for 25 dances.

Police in Glasgow were very strict about dancing partners, who were never allowed to be escorted home by dancers. Top dancers who could compete were in great demand. They were often booked for the whole afternoon or evening. That would mean that they had to dance 26 dances in the afternoon and 30 in the evening.

Ladies and gentlemen tended to arrive at the ballroom independently and partners were chosen for their ability to dance well rather than through any romantic attraction. All the top people in the city attended and sometimes royalty came to special functions.

By the late twenties, besides the Albert, there was the Imperial, the Locarno, the Plaza, the Dennistoun Palais, the Berkeley, Green's Playhouse, the F & F Palais, the Waldorf, the Norwood and the St Andrew's Halls.

Competitions were beginning to proliferate amongst the ballrooms themselves as well as on a national level. Farquhar MacRae described the scene as it was in 1928:

In 1928, with Jessie Chapman, I won the Quickstep/Charleston championship at the Imperial. Friends encouraged us to enter the final heat of the big Santos Casani competition in the Locarno. All the best dancers were in the Locarno and the competitors all had dinner suits. I just had my smart lounge suit but we entered and we won the heat.

For the finals I borrowed a dinner suit from an instructor at the Plaza. This was a big occasion – a £5,000 contest at stake. We danced and we came third. I was thrilled. The winners got a big cup, the runners-up got a cabinet gramophone and we each won a portable gramophone and records for being heat winners and a table grand gramophone and records each for coming third. I remember I had to hire a taxi to take us both home with our prizes – it cost me four shillings. We had danced five dances in the competition: the Waltz, Slow Fox Trot, Tango and Yale Blues. When I got home I put the two gramophones on at the same time, one playing 'It's Wonderful' and the other, 'Baby Face'.

Following that success, Farquhar was encouraged to enter the Scottish *Daily Record* Championships. This involved dancing a Waltz in one hall, a Fox Trot in another and gradually building up to the grand Finals in St Andrew's Halls.

It seemed wise to take a lesson from the top dancers in Glasgow at the time,

Amateur Ballroom Dancing Championship of Great Britain

PRIZES AWARDED IN DISTRICT HEATS AND FINALS—IN EACH DISTRICT

DISTRICT FINALS
SECOND PRIZES.

DISTRICT FINALS
FIRST PRIZE CUPS.

DISTRICT FINALS
THIRD PRIZES.

DISTRICT HEATS
FIRST PRIZES.

DISTRICT HEATS –THIRD PRIZES
CIGARETTE CASES FOR
LADIES & GENTLEMEN.

DISTRICT HEATS
SECOND PRIZES.

PRIZES AWARDED IN 96 DISTRICT HEATS AND FINALS.

DISTRICT HEATS.

Prizes for the First, Second and Third Heats at each Hall.

FIRST PRIZES —2 Columbia Portable Grafonolas, value £4 15 0 each, and Records to total value £5 5 0.

SECOND PRIZES—2 Columbia Portable Grafonolas, value £3 10 0 each, and Records to total value £4 4 0.

THIRD PRIZES —One each Lady's and Gentleman's Cigarette Cases, value £2 0 0 each

DISTRICT FINALS.

For the District Championships.

FIRST PRIZES —2 Silver Cups, £15 0 0 each.

SECOND PRIZES—2 Columbia Grafonolas, table grand, model No. 119, value £8 10 0 each, and Records to total value £9 9 0.

THIRD PRIZES —2 Columbia Grafonolas, table grand, model No. 117, value £6 10 0 each, and Records to total value £7 7 0.

THE TOTAL NUMBER OF PRIZE AWARDS REPRESENT
60 Silver Cups, 384 Columbia Grafonolas and 1,728 Columbia Records, and 144 Cigarette Cases.

Columbia prizes

Bobby Philp and Ella Scutts (winners of the Star professional championships in Blackpool in 1931) and from Alex Warren of the Albert. They all said that Farquhar had great potential and with this encouragement ringing in his ears he reached the finals with Jessie Chapman.

The judges were top names in ballroom dancing: F Ford, C Taylor, J Richardson and Josephine Bradley. On the evening of the competition the floor was so slippery that dancers were slipping all over the place. Farquhar had foreseen the problem and had brought rosin for their shoes so they were able to fly round the floor. 'We felt great. This was all fun. All the élite of Glasgow were there.'

Competing against them were Farquhar's idols, Alex McIntyre and Ethel Miller; and Mr A Sclanders and Miss J Fraser (rumoured to have taken £50 a time lessons from Josephine Bradley and very good dancers indeed).

In the event, Farquhar and Jessie came second. 'We were on top of the world. I won a dress watch for a white waistcoat.'

This success led to Farquhar becoming professional, and he was now asked to adjudicate competitions and give demonstrations with his partner.

He summed it up:

> The dancing standard was higher then in Glasgow than any other place in Britain. There will never be dancers again like the dancers of that time. Body movement, grace and deportment were all taught then and ballroom dancing was a cult.

For the top dancers this was a period of prosperity and hard work. They travelled all over the country giving dancing demonstrations. At a typical engagement at the Pavilion, Dunoon, they could earn a fee of five pounds but had to pay their own travel expenses. Spectators paid sixpence to watch from the balcony while dancers were charged two and sixpence.

George and Bertha Dundas, owners of the Dundee Palais, were delighted with the response when they invited Alex Warren and Betty McGregor, billed as Scotland's greatest ballroom dancers, to demonstrate their skills at the New Palais in December 1929. The *Dundee Telegraph* was full of praise for 'style developed to its highest degree and marvellously neat footwork'. Even a hard-bitten reporter was impressed enough to write,

> Mr Warren's appearance does not conform to the accepted idea of a professional dancer, and that is half the battle nowadays where good dancing is concerned. Tall and broad-shouldered, he has a real look of outdoors about him.[7]

Style was of the essence in ballroom dancing now. When one of the big eleven ballrooms in Glasgow, Green's Playhouse Ballroom, opened its doors officially in November 1928, it advertised itself as 'Absolutely the last word in Ballroom elegance . . . Treated in French Empire period – old gold and rose du Barry.' The ceiling boasted 1,000 lights and the floor was unique, a square of parquetry built on 1,000 springs. The ballroom was on the top floor of a building which housed a huge cinema. Dancers entered by lifts and there were more lifts to take them to a viewing balcony.

In less plush surroundings, it seems that a small ballroom at 38 Raeburn Place in Edinburgh had an unusual claim to fame. First owned by Peter Ogg in 1922 it was taken over by the dance teacher James A Mavor. In 1928 or 1929 it was renamed Palais de Plaisir and was run by what was then called 'the coloured community'. Locals remember that non-whites (probably Asians), were not welcomed into the city ballrooms at that time. In some ballrooms, like the Marine Gardens, young white girls were not permitted to dance with 'coloured men'. However, it was noted that the Palais de Plaisir employed some white dancing partners and the ballroom was run in exemplary fashion.

The twenties also brought big names in ragtime bands. Amongst the well-known musicians who played at the Albert, for instance, were George Chisholm, Tommy McQuater on trumpet, Dave Goldberg on guitar, Eric Spenser, Billy Miller on piano, Bill McGuffie and Hamish Christie.

Looking back over the twenties it is clear that the ballrooms had seen sweeping changes, perhaps more than at any other time. This is less surprising when taken in the context of a world which had also experienced massive changes as a direct result of the First World War. In every area there was an air of change and challenge. Transport was easier and faster by land, sea and now, by air. Cars were easy to run and relatively cheap to buy.

Women were emancipated, having been given the vote at the age of 30 in 1918 and at the age of 21 in 1928. With their new status they dared to raise hem levels from ground level to 12 inches from the ground by 1920. Their hairstyles had been transformed from the long tresses of previous centuries to the shingle of 1924 and the Eton Crop of 1925. Even the materials of their dresses had become easily manageable artificial silk and rayon, compared to the heavy linens and cottons of the past. They were using birth control and the smaller size of families would lead to more freedom in the way they passed their time.

For men, the picture was less rosy. There were new challenges and opportunities in the development of transport and industry for those who had work, but this was the decade of unemployment – 16.5% in 1921 – resulting in the General Strike of 1926 and over one million unemployed by 1928. Small wonder that for them the prospect of a few hours in the luxurious environment of the Palais de Danse was attractive.

There were other forms of entertainment which offered distractions with the spread of radio and films, especially the 'Talkies' that began in 1929, but, on the whole, ballroom dancing took these on board and continued to flourish. In 1923 the BBC began to include dance music in their programme of entertainment. By 1926 there were one million licence holders listening to Jack Payne and the London Radio Dance Band. When Ambrose broadcast from Mayfair in 1929 that figure had risen to a staggering 10 million. Listeners were invited to 'roll up the carpet and dance' and that is just what they did in their millions.

CHAPTER SIX

Big Bands and Scandals

∾ ∽

1930 to 1940

At the beginning of the thirties there were many people who, on the face of it, had little reason to dance. This was a time of major depression with unemployment reaching an all time high of three million in 1932. Hunger marchers made headline news and the country suffered in what was actually a pre-war period. The flappers of the twenties were replaced by more sober dancers who sported longer hair and lower hems and danced the standard dances in a sedate manner to sweet music.

In America, entrepreneurs took advantage of the popularity of dancing and in the misery of the Great Depression, they set up dance marathons. Men and women, desperate to earn money to support their families, were prepared to go through the physical and emotional torture of non-stop, dance-till-you drop competitions in the hope of winning money prizes. Onlookers paid to watch and sometimes even threw coins at the dancers. Contestants were subjected to painful endurance tests and were treated in many ways like performing animals.

It was reported that, in one marathon, the contestants danced for 22 weeks, three and a half days. They were permitted only 15 minutes rest in each hour which was reduced to three minutes during the last two weeks and there was no rest period at all during the final 52 hours. The final prize for the surviving couple was $1,000. A film, from the novel by Horace McCoy, *They Shoot Horses Don't They?* released in 1969, gives a graphic picture of the agonies of this kind of event.

Marathon dancing failed to catch on in Scotland although dancers remember that a limited version of it took place in the Marine Gardens in the early thirties.

Bert Valentine recalled what it was like in the north of Scotland. He first joined a band in Aboyne, Royal Deeside, in 1932 when he was fifteen. He played the piano, his brother played the violin and the saxophone and his father played the drums. Along with a friend who played guitar, this family band played at the Birst Lodge Hotel, Aboyne:

> At that time there were dances in every village hall but for special occasions there was the nightly dancing at the Palais de Danse in Aberdeen, 30 miles away. This was a very dressy affair. Men were expected to wear tails and the ladies wore evening dress. The favourite music of the time were the tunes: 'A Sin to Tell a Lie' and 'Whispering'. On the radio every night there were the top bands, Roy Fox, Harry Roy, Charlie Kunz, Jack Jackson, Sydney Kyte and Eddie Carroll.

The Valentine band became popular at functions in various private houses, mansion houses and castles in the north:

> We played 'Palais dances' in the main: Fox Trot, One Step, Quick Step, Waltz and Tango with the occasional Paul Jones but rarely Scottish Country Dances. At the private functions it was usual to include a Highland Schottische, Eightsome Reel, Lancers and Quadrilles. Occasionally, we would finish with a Galop. These programmes generally ran from 2.00 pm to 2.00 am.

A well-known band from Ballater, the Knowles, joined up with the Valentines on one occasion to play at a function at Balmoral Castle. On that evening, the Queen was represented by the Countess of Shaftesbury.

The band enjoyed regular work round the district and members of the band could generally count on a pound to one pound ten shillings per head per night for big functions and fifteen shillings for smaller local hops.

The Valentine family lived for ten years on the Glentanner Estate:

> Lord Glentanner had a huge ballroom in his mansion and a stage equivalent in size to the stage in London's Drury Lane. He could, and did, occasionally, engage the entire cast from a top London theatre and bring them up to the estate for a holiday. Sometimes he invited a top London orchestra to play in the ballroom.

This was the era of the big bands, whose leaders became household names as they were heard across the world on radio programmes. The bands developed individual styles and travelled all over the country to make guest appearances in the ever-growing number of Palais ballrooms.

The English Style of dancing was now firmly established, with the help of the husband and wife teams, the Vernon Castles and Victor Sylvesters, who were its greatest promoters and advocates. From the early thirties Exam Medal tests were inaugurated. Dancers could gain bronze, silver or gold medals as they progressed. This system was an immediate success and served to boost the classes of dancing teachers.

However, there was a growing trend for dancers to ignore the teachers and 'pick up' the dances as they went along. By the end of this period it was noticeable that the middle and upper classes in particular had largely given up dancing lessons and, as a result, the best dancers were to be found at the big, popular Palais, while the exclusive clubs and top hotels tended to attract dancers who merely shuffled through the motions.

The onset of war in September 1939 brought about the inevitable challenge and change to the status quo. In America there was a new vogue for Swing music which was a development from jazz made popular by Benny Goodman and his band in Hollywood. This was musician's music in which the bands followed the score while soloists improvised at intervals. The 'new' rhythms of Swing demanded new dances and they appeared, first as the Lindy Hop and then as the more popular Jitterbug.

As one writer puts it,

> The Jitterbug greatly increased the dynamic range of our social dancing. Some movements were very strong, indeed rough – the man pulling the girl towards him with one hand, and then twisting her round under his arm and then away again. But the important thing was the departure from the old ballroom close-hold to dancing with one's partner at arm's length. This was only a transitional stage leading to the complete separation of the partners.[1]

Swing might in fact have been transitory were it not for the war, when in the early forties Americans arrived in their thousands, bringing with them the latest steps in the Jitterbug. It was a fast, on the spot dance using acrobatic and highly dangerous movements which caused so much damage that some ballrooms banned it.

Another new dance made an early appearance in the ballrooms. The Rumba was of Afro-Cuban origin and was described as an 'erotic dance with violent and sinuous movements of hip, shoulder and torso.'[2] All important in the Rumba was the percussion rhythm. It was introduced by the Cuban band of Don Aspiazu who brought the dance to England and to what was a lukewarm reception in the thirties. In Scotland, in late 1931, the Rumba began to feature particularly at the Glasgow Plaza and the Edinburgh Fountainbridge Palais. In 1932, the Albert in Glasgow was still making a big feature of the Charleston while the Dennistoun Palais had demonstrations of the Rumba and the Charlestep. The Rumba really caught the imagination of the Scots and, in late 1932, Green's Playhouse in Glasgow reported that over 1,000 dancers had taken Rumba tuition there in the course of just two weeks.

A development of the Rumba, the Carioca, was demonstrated in the Albert by John Warren and partner in 1934. The dance caught on and was also featured in the Glasgow Playhouse and in Happy Valley in Edinburgh that year.

One other major trend at this time was a fondness for novelties, or participation social dances. These were simple dances involving the entire company in simple movements to lyrics reminiscent of children's party games. They were dances to keep up the spirits in the dark days of war and they were immensely and lastingly popular.

The Scottish Professional Champions, John Warren and Dorothy Dawn, at the Albert Ballroom in 1937

In 1937 Ida Lupino had a big hit with the musical, *Me and my Gal* in which the Lambeth Walk featured. This was published as C L Heimann's 'Novelty Dances Number 1' in 1937. It was a walking dance: 'side by side forward 8 steps; arms linked with partner, circle 8 steps; 2 steps forward, 3 quick steps forward (rpt); back 3 steps; slap knees; 3 forward steps; salute.'

'The Chestnut Tree', released on 15 November, 1938, matched words and actions to a simple melody along with a polka-like hop and a swing step:

> Underneath [point to floor] the spreading [arms wide] chest [touch chest] nut [touch head] tree [arms spread wide like branches], I loved her and she loved me, There she used to sit upon my knee . . .

'Knees Up Mother Brown' by Harris Weston and Bert Lee appeared on 12 December 1939. It was a song about a Pearly Queen party in London. In an energetic chorus, dancers combined Waltz steps with hip bumps and a knees-up trotting:

> Come along dearie, let it go, Ee i ee i ee i oh,
> It's your blooming birthday,
> Let's wake up all the town,
> Knees up, knees up, don't get the breeze up . . . . . .'

In 1939 Boomps-a-Daisy was the creation of Annette Mills, sister of the actor John Mills and former Charleston champion. Once again, the words were child-

A novelty race at the Marine Gardens. The starter with the white handkerchief was the assistant manager, Mr Tommy McCall

like and the actions followed the words interspersed with a combination of swing and walk steps: 'Hands [clap hands with partner], knees [partners slap own knees], and boomps-a-daisy [partners bump hips and bow].'

Two other enduring favourites were the Hokey Cokey (or Hokey Kokey) and the Palais Glide. The Hokey Cokey was a version of a children's action game. In a circle dancers performed the actions:

> You put your right hand in
> You put your right hand out
> You put your right hand in
> And you shake it all about.
> You do the Hokey Cokey [hands grasped, arms rocking]
> And you turn around
> That's what it's all about – Oi!

The Palais Glide was less of a game and more of a novelty dance. Arranged by Monsieur Pierre and Miss Doris Lavelle, London West End dance teachers, it was danced by one or by several couples in a line facing the same way and linked by arms round waists. This was a walking dance involving heel pointing and foot crossing in a progression across the ballroom. It began: 'Left heel forward to left; cross left foot behind right foot, step to side with right foot; cross left foot in front of right foot; repeat using opposite feet.' It sounds complicated but was simple enough in action and was danced to an amazing selection of music. The favourite was, 'Poor Little Angeline' but there was also, 'Old Folks at Home', 'Loch Lomond', 'John Brown's Body', 'Pop Goes the Weasel' and 'Il Trovatore'!

The Paul Jones was perhaps one of the most popular of all the novelty dances. It was often used as a warming up dance on occasions when the organisers wanted to mix partners and create a happy social atmosphere. The band often started with a bright tune like, 'Life on the Ocean Wave' or 'Here We Go Gathering Nuts in May'. The dancers formed two concentric circles with the men on the inside, facing out, and the women on the outside, facing in. With hands joined, the two circles moved to the right so that they were moving in different directions. When the music stopped, each man claimed the lady facing him as his partner. They danced to a Waltz, Quickstep or Fox Trot until the music stopped again and the dancers returned to the circle formation. This dance was particularly good because it included the whole company and nobody needed to be left out.

The Excuse Me dance was another method of mixing partners. In its early form, half a dozen men and women were given cards with 'Excuse Me' written on them. The band played, the company danced and the card holders stood in the middle of the floor. When the band stopped, the men presented their card to the partner of any dancer of their choice while the women could select any man and give his partner the card. The process was then repeated with the dispossessed partners holding the cards.

71

Later, the cards were dispensed with and everyone danced until the music stopped when any man could leave his partner and tap another man on the shoulder. The man had to give up his partner and find another one. A Double Excuse Me was a free-for-all when men or women could select new partners at the end of the music.

Private dances were often the highlight of the social calendar for working people and employers would choose these occasions to present prizes which were usually awarded to couples in novelty dances.

In the Spot Dance the organisers pre-selected certain 'spots' on the floor which were unmarked. Couples started to dance and when the music stopped everyone had to stand still. A spotlight was focussed on the 'spots' and the couple standing nearest to the spotlight was awarded the prize. In a variation of this, the band leader would be called to take a pattern of steps across the floor – '3 steps forward, 7 steps to the right, 5 steps forward . . .' – and the couple nearest him when he stopped won the prize.

Another popular prize dance was the Elimination Dance. When the floor was packed with dancers the band would stop playing and the bandleader would ask, for example, all ladies wearing blue to leave the floor with their partners. As numbers reduced the music would start again and each time the music stopped he would eliminate more. Gentlemen wearing bow ties; ladies with silver shoes; couples who have never met before this dance . . . The last couple on the floor won the prize.

The years between 1930 and 1940 were happy years, with new dances, new music and big bands. This time has been called the Golden Age of the Big Bands. The top bands were based mainly in London but the spread of radio enabled them to reach huge audiences all over the country. Top band leaders became superstars with enormous followings of fans. By 1933 there was dance music on the BBC regularly every day and every evening.

Scottish listeners had a particular reason to tune in to the BBC when, in 1932, against strong competition, the plum job of leader of the first BBC Dance Orchestra went to Henry Hall from 'Gleneagles'. The Gleneagles Hotel was the most famous of the chain of LMS Railway hotels. Henry Hall first formed his band there and had in fact first broadcast in 1924. His initial popularity led to his appointment as Musical Director for all the LMS Railway hotels. The music of the Henry Hall band was considered by some of his contemporaries to be somewhat bland in style, but he had a huge following amongst dancers. Along with his six-piece combo he moved to London and, rapidly, his became one of the best-known bands in the country.

Still prominent in the band scene in Glasgow was Louis Freeman who had supplied orchestras for picture houses in the twenties. He was now the Musical Director for the Anchor Line and the Donaldson Line, and supplied orchestras for the 20 shipping lines that sailed up the River Clyde. 'Louis Freeman's Navy' was so well established that it was said that if a musician didn't work for Louis Freeman, he didn't work.

Louis Freeman, bandleader and impresario, who died in March 1994 at the age of 101.
He played his last gig at the age of 99

Regular bands on the ships were usually trios, but, on the cruise ships, orchestras would have six or seven players. These were popular bookings for musicians. They earned nine pounds and ten shillings a month and the bandmaster would earn £11. However, on cruises, tips could treble the wages, and with little opportunity to spend, the men could come home with substantial savings. Later on the Musician's Union negotiated a deal with the Anchor Line and wages were increased to £14 but with no collections of tips.

One man who worked in Freeman's Navy, John McCormack, said,

Playing in the ships was a remarkable experience. I was just 17, out of school barely three years. The boys I had been to school with were working in factories and foundries

73

for about 10 shillings a week. I had £14 a month, all found, and the best of food, a table waiter, bedroom steward to look after me. It was really great for me at that age.

Louis Freeman was also active in the Glasgow Ballroom dancing scene in the thirties. He opened the Berkeley Ballroom and later, profits from that were used to open the Plaza. He was also appointed musical director of Green's Playhouse where he remained in charge for 35 years.

John McCormack had very early connections with ballroom orchestras. He began in Dundee. At his first engagement at the Tay Street Palais he sang a song called 'I've Had My Moments' – an unconvincing choice for a lad of 13! Billed as 'Little Mickey' he went on to play the piano four nights a week in the Hibs Hall, Glasgow, which had just opened in 1934. From there he progressed to the West End Ballroom, the Imperial, the Locarno and the massive Dennistoun Palais. It was said that in the Dennistoun Palais, eight times round the floor was a mile.

In the early thirties there were three big firms which supplied bands for functions and ballrooms all over Scotland. They were owned by Louis Freeman, Chalmers Wood and Pete Lowe. One young man, Andy Lothian, began to work for them, travelling round the country and gaining experience.

Andy had started his musical career playing for the silent movies in Glasgow cinemas. In 1929 he moved into the dance band business, playing the violin at

The band on board the *Dilwara*, a cruise ship built in 1936 by the P & O Line. Left to right: Tommy Dignan, drums; Andrew Bathgate, clarinet and bagpipes; Peter Pringle, piano. The *Dilwara* sailed during the Edinburgh and Glasgow Trades weeks from Leith to Stavanger, Bergen, Oslo and Copenhagen. It became a troop ship in 1939

Harry Smead and his Boys, Dundee Palais, 1932-33. Clem Stevens, trumpet; Hal Silcock, drums; Harry Smead; George Mointain; Vin Hamer, trombone; Sonny Lee, sax; Jack Reid, bass

private dance functions and also for Roger and Alice McEwan at their dance hall in Sauchiehall Street. For a time he joined his brother Carl's band, but decided to build up experience on his own. In 1933 he had a season in Edinburgh playing in a quartet in the restaurant of Binn's department store during the day, and transferring in the evening to the ballroom of the Royal British Hotel.

By 1937, Andy was leading a band in the Beach Ballroom in Aberdeen. In 1938 he led a band for six weeks at the Empire Exhibition in Glasgow. He followed this with a season at the Olympia Ballroom in Kirkcaldy where, in that lively season, there were visits from Joe Loss and Roy Fox.

On 28 October 1938 Andy and his band made a final move to the Dundee Palais where he was destined to spend 35 years on the bandstand. It was not easy at first. An earlier orchestra at the Palais led by Harry Smead had a devoted following. People would say, 'You're not bad, but, you're nothing like Harry Smead.'

1938 saw another change at the Palais when the tradition of supplying dancing partners was dropped.

In the early years, Cinderella dances were popular. Girls stood on one side of the floor and boys on the other. At about three minutes to midnight, the lights were lowered to a glimmer and each girl threw one of her dancing shoes into the middle of the floor. On the stroke of midnight, the cymbal beat twelve and the lights went up. This was the signal for all the boys to pick up a shoe and try to find the lady to match the shoe. When everyone had found a partner, they danced to the Cinderella Waltz.

Another novelty dance involved partners exchanging clothing at each break in the music. Ladies would wear gentlemen's jackets and shoes and ties; men would wear ladies' shoes or gloves. At the final stage, it was announced that whoever reached the bandstand properly dressed in their own clothes would win a prize.

A famous ballroom opened its doors in Glasgow on Christmas Eve 1934. Barrowland was built over a street market called the Barras, owned by the McIver family. It was the idea of Mrs Margaret McIver who had been widowed in the war. A young drummer in the band on that opening evening, Billy MacGregor, was destined to be responsible in great measure for the success of the venture. At the beginning of the war, in 1939, he took over the resident band, The Gaybirds, and was soon to be dubbed 'King Showman' in a business where competition was fierce.

Dancing in Barrowland was fun. On a small stage alongside the bandstand, Billy and the band would present sketches and comedy acts. Scripts for these were written by an old-time music hall favourite, Wullie Lindsay. No longer able to present his own acts, Wullie provided fresh scripts for Barrowland each week. Billy MacGregor, ably supported by the band, presented the scripts with flair and enthusiasm. In a workshop in the ballroom he constructed props and costumes. Every Saturday night, dancers could enjoy a new variety act. Billy might be a dashing private-eye called Billy Barton; he might saw a girl in half; he would stage a memory act; or he would be a potty psychiatrist hypnotising clients in outrageous routines. The dancers loved it.

They also loved to dance and packed in as many as 2,000 to 3,000 a night to dance to the rhythm of The Gaybirds band with Jimmy Phillips, Bobby Nicholson, Johnny McGinnes and Sanny Hosie on sax; John McVey, Snowy Deans, Jimmy Armstrong and Morris Deans on bass; Al Davenport on double bass; and Johnny Ruthven on piano.

Billy MacGregor recalled:

> From the start it was a great place to work. The McIvers were good bosses and great businessmen. They ran Barrowland in a different way from other ballroom owners. Since they didn't know a Quadrille from a Tango they left the bandleader in complete charge of the ballroom and when I took over as leader I enjoyed the freedom to make decisions.

The McIvers' lack of musical know-how was legendary. The story is told that Bert Cooper, the trombone player, had made an arrangement for the band. Mr McIver came to listen to the new arrangement and found three trumpet players sitting with their trumpets on their laps. He said to Cooper, 'Why are they no' playin'?' Cooper told him, 'They've got eight bars rest.' That wasn't good enough. McIver said, 'I don't pay them to rest. You write somethin' in for them.'

Billy Macgregor loved his work in Barrowland:

Matt Lind of the Colorado Band in the thirties at the Edinburgh Plaza

These were the easy years. Dancing was so popular you only had to open your doors and the crowds came. We did seven dances per hour for two to three hour sessions. We played the Fox Trot, (the Slow Fox Trot died in the early thirties) Quickstep, Tango, Rumba, and Waltz and repeated the Fox Trot and Quickstep. When a dancer had a 21st birthday we always presented a big silver cardboard key that opened up to show photos of the band.

This was a busy time for all the ballrooms. Bobby Jones ran the Berkeley and then moved to St Andrew's Halls where there were two ballrooms on the top floor: 'They were open from Saturdays to Mondays. The Norwood was a beautiful ballroom, small and intimate. They had a London band there and a Scottish band. It was always very select.'

At this time there was a strange phenomenon in some of the smaller Glasgow ballrooms. It was called 'Birling'. Banned in many halls because of the space it demanded, there were many versions but the most common was done to the music of 'Moonlight and Roses' played at a very fast speed. Partners leaned their heads on each other's shoulders and they 'birled' round very fast with coat tails flying.

Music for the big ballrooms was invariably provided by a regular resident band or orchestra with anything from four to sixteen players. Each band developed a personality – a unique blend of rhythm, tempo and style that combined with the idiosyncrasies of the resident dancing teacher to set the style of the ballroom. As an artist can recognise the works of fellow artists, dancers could always tell which ballroom other dancers visited most frequently by the style of their dancing. (The story is told that some dancers from Kirkcaldy were nicknamed 'Currie's Jumpers' because the dance floor where they practised was so small that they had developed a vertical rather than horizontal style.)

Some bands were known for their liveliness or brand of humour. One of the most popular Edinburgh Plaza bands was The Colorado led by George McIntosh with Matt Lind on saxophone and Jock Herbertson on violin. Every Saturday night Matt and Jock performed a parody of the 'Flanagan and Allen' act:

> Strolling thro' the Meadows
> Along the Whalebone Walk
> Strolling thro' the Meadows
> Of work we never talk
> That is where you'll find us
> On our daily stroll
> Patiently awaiting each Friday
> When we draw the dole
> Sleeping in the shelters
> Lying in the grass
> Watching the cops wot pass
> Spotting all the winners
> Nearly every day
> Strolling thro' the Meadows
> We're unemployed – Hurray!

The Plaza also had traditional ceremonies at New Year. On the last night of the year, a radio was brought to the centre of the main ballroom and a member of the band, dressed as Old Father Time, waited beside it. On the stroke of midnight, the doormen jostled him about the hall before throwing him out. In his place they brought the New Year Fairy (another member of the band) followed by a piper who piped in the New Year from the stage.

In 1933, Phil Richardson's Band was popular at the Fountainbridge Palais. In 1930 the gallery was opened to non-dancers to watch the tea-dancers in the afternoon. One of the early attractions was a fountain in the middle of the floor. The *Scottish Dancing Journal* reported in March 1934:

Tommy Meek and Mike Imrie, the doormen at the Edinburgh Plaza in 1933

Phil Richardson and his band are always bright and full of go. While rendering the Dashing White Sergeant it is not unusual for Phil and the boys to march in single file from the platform round and round the fountain with saxophones, trumpets, piano accordions and all except the double bass and grand piano.

The Glasgow Plaza also boasted a fountain in the middle of the floor and dancers had to learn that they were liable to be sprinkled with drops of water if they strayed too near it.

The Fountainbridge Palais in Edinburgh was run by a private company, Lucas and Son. In 1937 a new company was formed, the Edinburgh Dance Halls Ltd, run by Alan Fairley and Mr Heimann, who leased the property which was taken over again in November by Mecca. Major changes included the installation of a huge revolving stage and a new balcony. The new stage allowed space for two bands to follow one another without a break and the business of revolving the stage became a big attraction with dancers waving farewell to the retiring band and welcoming the new arrivals. John Holton's band at this time incorporated a Hammond electric organ which was new to Scotland. Another novelty in the ball-room then was an American Soda Fountain.

Among notable band leaders in Glasgow were Jack Chapman of the Albert, and Alex Freer of the Plaza. Another wonderfully versatile musician with a huge repertoire of music was Symon Stungo who worked with Louis Freeman making early recordings in 1934.

Many smaller towns in Scotland had a band that played for the Saturday night ballroom dancing in the local hall. As a result, band contests became popular. There were East of Scotland, West of Scotland and finally Scottish Amateur Dance Bands contests. The results were unpredictable with prizes often awarded to bands from smaller towns. Being a big city band was no guarantee of success. For example, in 1934, in the contest held in the Fountainbridge Palais, the winners were:

1st – Johnny Dick's Band from Happy Valley, Edinburgh
2nd – Imperial Dance band, Alloa
3rd – The Waverley Band, Edinburgh
4th – The Savoy Band, Kirkcaldy.

Bands often moved from ballroom to ballroom and many band players were freelance, moving to one-night 'gigs' as the opportunity arose. The music shop in Edinburgh, Methven Simpsons, ran a band-hire service. With several bands and a string of individual musicians on their books they could offer a variety of groups and styles.

Through radio broadcasts, the big bands which were based in the south of England and in the large resort Palais had become household names along with the handful of international bands, most of which came from America. In this golden era of bands, crowds flocked to see their favourites perform live during countrywide tours. Theatre managements had, for some time, been struggling to fill the one-time favourite Music Hall shows or Variety Shows as they were now

Joe Loss, the leader of one of the last of the big bands. Joe died in June 1990
(*by kind permission of Joe Loss Ltd*)

called. Cashing in on the success of the big bands, theatres invited them to appear as top of the bill and fans flocked to see them.

It became customary for bands to complete their engagements in the theatres and move on to the big ballrooms later in the evening for late-night dancing. In Edinburgh, the Empire Theatre would book a big band as top of the bill following a series of short variety acts. When the theatre closed, the band would move to the Marine Gardens, the Fountainbridge Palais, the Dunedin or the Eldorado for a late evening engagement from 10.30 pm to 4.00 am.

In Glasgow, bands would move from the Alhambra Theatre to the Plaza, the Playhouse or Barrowland ballrooms. Henry Hall, Roy Fox, Billy Ternant, Jack Hylton, Joe Loss and many others visited the cities of Glasgow and Edinburgh to play for their fans.

Joe Loss and his band started coming to Glasgow in 1936 when he played at the Dennistoun Palais. The following year he came back to the Pavilion Theatre and discovered that across the road, Green's Playhouse, then the biggest cinema in Europe, had a huge, empty room at the top of the building. For the next 17 consecutive years, he and his band brought in Hogmanay at Green's Playhouse which had become one of the most popular ballrooms in the city, despite the fact that entry was by lift to the top floor and the fire hazard must have been considerable. Joe Loss and his band also forged a strong link with the Plaza and he continued his annual visit to the Plaza right up to his death in 1990.

In the early thirties, few bands had vocalists but cabaret acts would entertain during the evening. One young soldier, based in the barracks near Portobello, was tempted to sing in a contest one day at Andrew Letta's Pierrot Show on the promenade. In true theatrical tradition, he was spotted by the assistant manager of the Marine Gardens Ballroom, Mr Tommy McCall, who had taken a stroll between dancing sessions. Mr McCall invited him to sing with the band that evening and, before long, he was singing there regularly. Taking the advice of Mr McCall, the young soldier chose a song he found in the Music Arcade in Princes Street as his signature tune. The song was 'By a Babbling Brook' and the soldier was Donald Peers who became world famous as a top singer.

Crooners were beginning to interest the dancers, especially when the big bands began to tour and BBC broadcasts made them familiar figures. Crooning contests were held occasionally in the ballrooms when aspiring crooners could attempt to copy the top names of the day: Sam Costa with Lew Stone's band; Vera Lynn with Ambrose; and Al Bowly, the top vocalist who sang with many bands.

Ballroom dancing was a very respectable and popular pursuit but the decade had its scandals, mainly associated with the dance clubs. There were rumbles of trouble in the early thirties as authorities tried to bring clubs under the much stricter by-laws relating to the ballrooms.

Clubs were open to members only, but the cost of membership might be a token amount and, in some cases, involved no more than a signature in a book. Clubs also kept later hours on a regular basis compared to ballrooms, where late dances were reserved for special after-theatre visits from big bands. For example, Edinburgh's Havana Club in Princes Street was open nightly from 10.30 pm to 4.00 am except for Saturdays, when it had to close before midnight. One dancer recalled that you had to knock on a door and an aperture in the door was opened so that you could be scrutinised before being allowed to enter.

Another complication was that clubs were licensed, while no ballroom at that time was permitted to sell alcohol. Glasgow was generally regarded as being stricter about dancing regulations than Edinburgh. Be that as it may, it is true that the major scandal of the decade occurred in the capital city.

The scandal was caused by the misuse of dancing partners. By the mid-thirties, dancing partners were being phased out by the big Palais ballrooms in favour of demonstration or exhibition couples. Many of the bigger ballrooms now had a school of dancing with a qualified dance teacher in charge. Where dancing partners were employed, the big ballrooms tended to adhere strictly to the rules.

In the clubs, however, customers frequently required partners. The famous song, 'Ten Cents a Dance' is a reminder of the hard workers of the dancing world. The charge was usually sixpence a dance of which the management kept fourpence. Usually, girls employed as partners were expected to supply their own dresses and shoes although the latter were often gifted by grateful clients.

When a girl earned for herself twopence a dance, her top earnings for a day and night would be 10 shillings for 60 dances. Of course, on the nights when the club was booked by a private party, the girls did not earn a penny.

It was common knowledge that in some clubs it had become the practice of unscrupulous managements to 'book out' a partner for an hour at a total cost of thirty shillings. Girls, lured to the city by promises of a glamorous job, might find it difficult to pay for digs,food and clothes and the pressure must have been considerable to fall into this form of prostitution.

It must be said that, in the majority of respectable clubs and dance halls, partners were never allowed to leave the premises during working hours and clients were strictly forbidden to walk home with partners.

Glasgow magistrates, as early as 1927, had passed by-laws relating to dance halls which led to the accusing headlines, 'Grandmotherly Glasgow', in the *Sunday Post*. In Glasgow, instructors had to remain on the premises from 7 pm to 11.30 pm and particulars of their days off had to be furnished to the police if necessary. No lady could enter a dance hall unless accompanied by a gentleman. Partners could not be booked for more than one dance at a time and were not allowed to fraternise with patrons or sit at tables with them. Partners were to be taken in strict rotation and dances paid for in advance, one at a time.

There were squeals of indignation from Glasgow dancers who protested that their ballrooms were least in need of such restrictions. The magistrates replied that these were measures to prevent 'booking out' which had occurred in Edinburgh. They were determined that such practices should not happen in Glasgow but left it up to the managements of the various ballrooms in the city to exercise their own discretion when applying the new stringent by-laws.

The situation in Edinburgh was causing concern, however, and that scourge of immorality, forerunner of Mary Whitehouse, Edinburgh policeman William Merrilees, was determined to clean up the problem in the city.

William Merrilees was a small man with a big reputation. He targeted the Kosmo Club, the oldest established dancing club in Edinburgh. Opened in Swinton Row in 1923 by Mr Asher Barnard, the club had been called the Bohemian Club originally and was immensely popular. In 1928 the name was changed to the Kosmo Dance Club. Despite constant surveillance and strong suspicions it seemed impossible to prove that a club frequented by the top people in the city could be connected in any way with shady business.

The premises consisted of a fair-sized dancing hall with a lesser darkened hall curtained off at one end from which there were two exits – one through an adjoining garage owned by Mr Barnard. On the face of it, business continued normally and the June edition of the *Dancing Times* magazine reported that, 'The Kosmo Dance Club remains open every night for dancing and, owing to its central position and well-appointed premises, its membership roll is constantly increasing.'

The night of the big police raid was Monday 25 July 1933. Merrilees' description of the stake-out is reminiscent of a prohibition raid on a Speakeasy. The club was already in full swing with 150 dancers on the floor. The building was surrounded. Police moved in and Mr Barnard, the manager, was charged and arrested. The Kosmo closed, never to open again.

The subsequent trial so shocked the judge that he said he regretted that details must be made public. It seemed that there was ample proof of guilt and Barnard was sentenced to 18 months imprisonment for living off immoral earnings.

The second scandal, also centred in Edinburgh, was an equally flamboyant affair. One of the more popular ballrooms in the city was Maxime's at Tollcross. Opened in November 1921, it had done tremendous business under the management of Mr F S Simpson. The building had been a riding stables originally until Mr Peter Ogg and his two sisters took it over after the First World War as the Grafton Café. The building had little windows where feed for horses had been kept and there were iron rings on the walls to tie up the horses.

In October 1921 the building had been renamed Maxime's. The press reported that there would open shortly a beautiful new Dancing Salon at Tollcross. In November, the Grand Opening Ball revealed a Japanese lounge, French and Turkish rooms and a Winter Garden. Dancers danced to the music of two London bands. Admission was seven shillings and sixpence. Evening or dinner dress was required.

Maxime's flourished. There were charity balls, amateur championships and visiting cabaret artistes, for instance, Mark Griver, 'the singing banjoist'. A new band arrived in 1931 led by Mr Harry Thorley. In November that year they celebrated the 10th anniversary of the ballroom with a Carnival Ball attended by 400 dancers. (The Tango was the most popular dance of the evening.)

This was a ballroom that went in for gimmicks. Friday nights were novelty nights when 'bonuses' of £5, £4, £3, £2 and £1 were given away. Maxwell Stewart and Pat Sykes were engaged from London to demonstrate the Tango and the Skater's Waltz. Wednesdays were 'Free Excursion Nights' when couples could win two tickets to almost any town in Scotland or the north of England. Vouchers were given to each dancer on entry and the owners of the lucky numbers would win cash prizes.

The winter of 1932 brought disaster. The *Dancing Times* reported, 'With the complete destruction of Maxime's by fire, dancers have lost a real "home from home". It is hoped to rebuild and re-open before Christmas . . .'

In the event, it was 27 September 1933 when Maxime's held the Grand Re-opening Ball. Mr Ogg had taken the chance to rebuild on an even grander scale. £20,000 was spent on the new building. There were walls of mirrors and walls covered with vellum. The Lord Provost attended and all proceeds on that opening night went to the Royal Infirmary.

The 'ballroom of 1,200 lights' was back in business with dancing from 8 pm to

1.30 am. Amongst the attractions were settees set round the special 'spring floor' where dancers could sit and enjoy the music of Harry Thorley's band.

The scandal, when it came, was sudden and devastating. The new ballroom was a tremendous success, attracting top bands, top teachers and top dancers. Unfortunately, it also gathered a reputation for homosexual activities. An assistant at the ballroom, Ewan King, was nicknamed 'the Pansy King'. The policeman William Merrilees determined to stamp out what was at that time an illegal practice. Some people might say that his methods of investigation were questionable. Ewan King owned a bed and breakfast establishment in town and, in order to gather 'evidence' Merrilees broke into the property, stole a key from a purse, had it copied and returned it. He later used the key to gain access to the building and hid in a cupboard to listen to what was being said in an adjoining room.

There was a dramatic police raid and Maxime's was closed on 12 April 1938. In the *Dancing Times* there was an untypically cryptic announcement: 'Maximes Ballroom at Tollcross held its last session for public dancing on Tuesday April 12th 1938'. No doubt, 'nuff said.

In a subsequent trial, despite the dubious methods of obtaining 'evidence', the police obtained convictions. It seems extraordinary now that the ballroom should have been closed when a change of management might have been adequate to stamp out the practices of a few offenders. On the other hand, perhaps draconian measures were required to bring the scandal to a satisfactory conclusion.

Scandal or no, this was not to be the end of this remarkable building. It was taken over and re-opened under a new name – the Cavendish. This business venture was short-lived but was followed up by a second rescue, this time by Mr Tim Wright. He knew all about the ballroom business, having a successful band of his own. The new premises, renamed 'the New Cavendish', quickly established a good reputation and the business flourished.

There were now four established dances, the Waltz, the Fox Trot, the Quickstep and the Tango. However, the split was increasing between 'crush' or 'rhythm' dancers who saw dancing as a purely social activity and 'Palais'-style, competitive dancers who saw it as a skill. Part of the problem was space. Competitive dancing required spacious floors with only a few dancers performing at any one time. The fact remained that most people wanted to dance rather than spectate. As a result, in general, most of the smaller towns favoured social dancing. In Dundee, for instance, there were few serious competitions although the town had several ballrooms.

In the main, the big competitions centred on Glasgow and Edinburgh while the pre-final heats could be held in dance halls all over Scotland. Inter-city competitions between Glasgow and Edinburgh allowed them to exercise their old rivalry, with Glasgow claiming victory consistently throughout the thirties. Small, in-house championships had been taking place in ballrooms for some time, usually associated with a particular dance.

Alex Warren had fulfilled his promise to his father to make the Albert prominent on the dancing map. He widened the scope of competition when he inaugurated the West of Scotland Championships in 1925. These were followed, inevitably, by the East of Scotland Championships. In the east there was also the Edinburgh League, an in-city competition for eight local ballrooms: Happy Valley, Locarno, Excelsior, Eldorado, New Dunedin, Macdonald's, Piershill and the Victoria.

In 1928, the Locarno in Glasgow hosted the first Scottish Professional Championships organised by the *Daily Record* and won by Mr Alex Warren and Miss Cecilia Bristow. Also that year, the Columbia Gramophone Company instituted the Amateur Ballroom Championship of Great Britain, and Scottish heats for that were held in the Marine Gardens, Portobello.

Now, in the thirties, having won a clutch of prizes between 1929 and 1933, Alex Warren decided to give up competitive dancing to continue as promoter, patron and adjudicator. His first concern was to pull together the ballroom dance teachers in Scotland. Accordingly, he founded the Scottish Dance Teacher's Alliance at the Albert on 18 August 1934. He also helped to found the Scottish Ballrooms Association which looked after the interests of the big ballrooms.

Some ballrooms held their own championships and there were the Mecca Gold Cup Contests in the late thirties. Perhaps the most bizarre were the

Fifeshire finals of the Scottish Dancing Championship held in the Masonic Hall, Kirkcaldy, 30 November 1935. Prizes were gold wristlet watches. Mrs T Johnston is presenting prizes to the winners judged by Miss Anne Warren (first on right)

Alex Warren in 1931

Glasgow Bantam Championships held in the Imperial Ballroom in the late thirties and restricted to contestants below a certain height.

During this decade there was some concern in Scottish Country Dance circles that the traditional dances were no longer popular with the dancing masses in the ballrooms. A radio appeal by the Scottish Country Dance Society asking ballrooms to include old Scottish dances like the Triumph, Petronella, Flowers of Edinburgh and the Glasgow Highlanders in their programmes largely fell on deaf ears. Most palais ballrooms concentrated on modern dances with the occasional Eightsome Reel thrown in as a speciality. 'Old Time' enthusiasts were catered for on separate nights. For example, the Marine Gardens had Old Time on Mondays and Fridays; modern dancing on Tuesdays and Saturdays; and roller-skating on Thursday evenings and Saturday afternoons. (Keen dancers always complained that the roller-skating damaged the floor.)

At the top of the ballroom dance world in Scotland there were a few couples who were outstanding. They toured the ballrooms to give demonstrations and all of these dancers became dance teachers. Teaching ballroom dancing was big business in the thirties.

1936 saw the beginning of another dancing phenomenon – formation dancing. One of the first formation dance teams was formed at the New Locarno in Glasgow. A very special team was formed in Glasgow in 1937, Coronation year. A team formed by the top Scottish professional ballroom dancers was sponsored by the *Daily Record*. Seven top Glasgow ballrooms became involved and it was arranged that the team would dance in each ballroom in turn on Coronation Day travelling from one to another in a small bus. The dancers were: John Warren and Dorothy Dawn, Duncan McKellar and Betty McGregor, Bobby Philp and Ella Scutts, and Alex Warren and Anne Warren.

The newly formed committee of the Scottish Dance Teachers' Alliance. From left to right, back row: Mr J Stewart, Miss A McEwan, Miss Nancy Munro, Miss Stuart Johnstone, Mr Roger McEwan; front row: Mr Alex Warren, Mrs Bankhead, Mr J A Diamond, Miss Marjorie Middleton and Mr Alex McIntosh.
(*Courtesy of the* Dancing Times)

The Coronation Dance Team of Scottish Ballroom Champions. From left to right: John Warren, Dorothy Dawn, D McKellar, Betty McGregor, Ella Scutts, R H Philp, Anne Warren, Alex Warren

Billy MacGregor remembered the arrangements well: 'They rehearsed in Barrowland in the afternoon and we were the first ballroom to see their beautiful routine that evening. From us they went to the Dennistoun Palais, then the Plaza, Green's Playhouse, the New Locarno, West End Ballroom and finished up at the Albert.' That night they recorded a total of 8,000 dancers who cheered on the Formation Dance Team and they later appeared at the final of the Scottish National Dancing Championships that year when Sir Harry Lauder was a guest.

Edinburgh dancers were also involved in Coronation revels in a big way. There was a Coronation Gala at the Picadilly Club, late nights all week at the Fountainbridge Palais and a huge Coronation Ball at the Marine Gardens from 9.00 pm to 3.00 am. A special train was run from Glasgow for the occasion.

Glasgow had something else to celebrate when, in March 1938, the huge Empire Exhibition opened in Bellahouston Park. One of the attractions at the exhibition was a specially built ballroom to accommodate 300 dancers. Though small in capacity, the ballroom was perpetually busy under the management of the experienced Alex Warren. The Empire Exhibition was an enormous draw. On the first Saturday 195,000 people visited the park. Those privileged few who could find a space on the small dance floor danced to the music of Bobby Hind and his London Sonora band, a big 17-piece combo.

September '38 saw the opening of yet another ballroom in Edinburgh. Owned by entrepreneur David Sharp, the Silver Slipper had to come up with something special to attract custom from the Plaza, already well-established across the road. The Edinburgh *Evening News* reported the opening:

> The ballroom has a novelty in the shape of tables which contain tanks of goldfish covered with plate glass tops . . . . At the entrance is a huge barrel-shaped cage in which several canaries add their voice to the sound of music above . . .

Well, it was different!

1938 was a significant year for dancers in Dundee. At that time the main ballrooms there were the Palais, Locarno and the West End Palais. There was also the Chalet in nearby Broughty Ferry. Saturday dances were held in Kidd's Rooms and there was a Café Dansant at Green's Playhouse. However, following the Empire Exhibition, the Duncan family brought a new ballroom to the city – the Empress. The building, erected at Royal Arch, Shore Terrace, was actually the stand for the Dominion of Canada which was removed from the Empire Exhibition lock stock and barrel.

THE PALAIS
31 SOUTH TAY ST.
DUNDEE

THE HOME OF DANCING AND DANCE TUITION
GEORGE DUNDAS AND BERTHA WILSON

George Dundas and Bertha Wilson, owners of the Dundee Palais.

The Excelsior Ballroom in Edinburgh. Behind the mike is the manager at that time,
Andrew Moffatt. The Excelsior was in St Cecilia's hall, currently one of Edinburgh's
oldest and most elegant concert halls (*With thanks to* The Courier, *Dundee*)

In 1938, Swing was the thing in Dundee. At the new Empress, Tom Finnie and
his New Trek were billed as the 'Masters of Swing'. Dancers were invited there
to 'Swing to Lionel Ray and his band – the answer to the Swing fan's prayer'.

There was another important date for Alex Warren in 1938 when he was
invited to New York as a ballroom champion to visit the famous 'Roseland', the
biggest ballroom in the world. There he was impressed by the '50 glamorous
instructresses in attendance'. In the Albert they had only ten instructresses at
that time. Alex was always very proud of the Albert. He claimed that 'People
there were always very good-mannered. Never a drunk crossed my door. I had
three uniformed attendants at the entrance but no bouncers. If anyone had to be
thrown out I did that myself.' (He was well qualified to do so as an ex-boxer and
one-time football player for Queen's Park Amateurs.) He said, 'It used to make
me very proud that some young girls were allowed to dance only at the Albert
and nowhere else because it was so well conducted.'

It seemed that in the season 1938 to '39 the Scottish dance world was buzzing.
All the resort ballrooms were registering record business. Aberdeen Beach
Ballroom, Aberdeen Palais, Marine Gardens and Ayr Pavilion were the biggest
ones outside Glasgow but everywhere was busy.

That summer, the Rothesay Pavilion was only one year old. Built to accommodate 700 dancers, it had a cafe with open-air tea balconies and a total capacity of 1,500. The favourite dances there that summer were the Handsome Territorial and Boomps-a-Daisy.

In November 1938, the Locarno, Glasgow was:

> proud to announce the Grand National Premiere of 'Chestnut Tree', a new novelty singing dance which is being presented simultaneously in all the leading ballrooms in Britain. Hear it on the wireless. It will sweep the country.

At the same time, the Dundee Palais was holding the first heat of the Ballito Tango competition, while in the Glasgow Locarno there was the final Bantam Championship judged by Bobby Philp and Ella Scutts.

This was a period when gimmicks were used to attract customers. The Palais, Dundee, ran a 'free presentation watch' promotion in which every lady and gentleman was presented with a watch on the occasion of their eighth visit. Various commercial firms ran big promotion dances at the Palais. Outdoor Girl, Cyclamen, Palmolive and Phillips Dental Magnesia all gave away free samples; Icilma handed out gift boxes of their cosmetics for every lady; on Nufix night, every gentleman took home a full-sized tube of Nufix tonic hair-dressing; Black and White Whisky gave away black and white doggy brooches; there was perfume on offer from 4711 and Evening in Paris; Brylcreem and Mars both had evening dances when dancers doubtless took home free samples.

Andy Lothian's band in Dundee

Contests were another major feature of the dance halls and in February 1939 the Palais held a Pygmalion Week in which ladies were invited to compete in a 'Flower-girl to Duchess' contest for which the top prize was a beautiful evening gown.

In March there was a challenging advert for a Jitterbug Contest at the Palais in conjunction with the Palace Theatre. After demonstrations of jitterbugging from the theatre company dancers, patrons of the ballroom were invited to 'Go to Town. Try Our Contest. Nothing Barred'.

One tradition, peculiar to the Dundee Palais, was known locally as 'the Monkey Walk'. On Sundays in Scotland, dancing was not permitted. Instead, the orchestras usually gave concerts. Andy Lothian's band gave a regular Sunday concert but, instead of sitting at tables to listen, couples promenaded round the ballroom. Always keeping to the right, the promenade would halt briefly during episodes of talent competitions and would then continue as soon as the band began to play again. At 9.00 pm, promenaders would parade out of the ballroom, up South Tay Street, turn right into Overgate, right down Lindsay Street, past Kidd's Rooms and right again into Nethergate, from where at about 10.30 pm they dispersed and went home.

In June and July 1939, the big city ballrooms were undergoing their summer re-decoration and several were extending to cope with the expected influx of dancers after the holidays. At the Albert, Alex Warren was preparing for the start of a revived West of Scotland Championship planned for October.

The announcement of the outbreak of war on 3 September 1939 put a stop to everything for a while. For a few weeks the country seemed to hold its breath. However, after the first shock of war was over, it was recognised that entertainment was needed now as never before. Restrictions were lifted on the opening of all entertainment houses. On 16 September, most of the ballrooms re-opened. It seemed as if there was a conscious effort to entertain during the war. War-time nerves could be stilled by attending evenings billed as 'Carefree', 'Go-As-You-Please', 'Rag-time Ball' and 'Carnival Gala'.

There were some differences, of course. Black-out restrictions made Matinee Dances and Tea Dances more popular. Evening sessions were shorter, from 7.00 pm to 10.00 pm. Boys tended to collect partners from home and return them safely to their doors instead of a more casual arrangement to meet them in the ballroom. Some dancers carried torches in their pockets in case the lighting failed. Andy Lothian recalled that during an air raid the ballroom electricity supply was hit and all the lights went out. Dancers and band solemnly lit their torches and carried on dancing and playing. .

There were casualties of another kind. The West of Scotland Championships were cancelled, Ayr Pavilion was closed, regular Saturday dances in provincial town halls had to be discontinued as halls were taken over for military purposes and, perhaps the greatest loss, the Marine Gardens was taken over by the Government and never opened again as a ballroom.

The Glasgow Plaza broke a long tradition. Friday nights had always been restricted to 'Evening Dress only'. With the outbreak of war, the management tried, as an experiment, to allow informal dresswear. After a few weeks the experiment was discontinued and tradition was restored with a minor alteration. Dancers must wear either evening dress or uniform.

As call-up papers arrived, familiar faces began to disappear from the scene. Lionel Ray and Jimmy Lothian went to war and their places in Dundee were filled by newcomers. Alex Warren was commissioned in the RASC and saw most of his service abroad while his brother John looked after the business at home.

By October 1939 ballrooms were advising all patrons that, to be admitted, they must be in possession of a gas mask.

Despite the times, spirits were still high. In December, dancers were introduced to a new dance at the opening night of the New Locarno in Dundee. It was called the Black-out Stroll, a novelty in which dancers found a new partner at intermittent black-outs during the dance.

Typical of the attitude of the age, the Fountainbridge Palais announced a 'Let's Be Cheerful Week' in 1940. On Thursday evening all patrons wearing uniforms were admitted for half price and on Friday, entry was free for members of the RAF.

At least one ballroom in Glasgow achieved recognition from overseas during the War – although it would have preferred to do without it. Lord HawHaw was an infamous German propagandist who broadcast on the 'wireless' at intervals during the hostilities with the intention of lowering morale. One night he announced that the Germans knew of a local landmark, an illuminated sign of a man wheeling a barrow on the roof of Barrowland. It was a veiled threat that the authorities decided to take seriously. It was considered wise to remove the sign.

Dancing in the 1930s had weathered scandals and pre-War nerves absorbing changes along the way. The biggest change in dancing came through the notorious Jitterbug. Franks said that the Jitterbug 'appalled parents pre the Second World War'[3] but, Victor Sylvester claimed, 'I tamed it into Jive which was a more acceptable form.'[4] It was certainly the dance which began the trend towards dancing independently of a partner.

Another change, brought about by the War, concerned dress. The outbreak of the Second World War meant that silk chiffon, the most favoured material in the thirties, became unobtainable. People had to accept clothes rationing and everyone was issued with coupons. One of the few materials that was not rationed was net. The net was made of rayon and was similar in texture to the nylon net we have today. Net had one drawback, which was that it did not hang and flow like silk chiffon. The solution to this was to make skirts wider and employ several layers, producing the bouffant effect which was to become the standard image of the female ballroom dancer.

The War brought about a change in attitude to dancing and to dancing partners which was to become more marked in succeeding years.

CHAPTER SEVEN

Crooners and Championships

∾ ∾

1940 to 1950

The war of 1939–1945 had a different effect on the population from the previous war of 1914–1918. The general feeling was less jingoistic. Families, not yet fully recovered from the losses in the first War, were inclined to cling together, stand firm and hope for an early peace. Singers like Frank Sinatra and Vera Lynn caught the mood of sentimentality, as did the big bands. There was a second strand in the public mood. It was a need for humour. Bands which could come up with a combination of sentimentality and humour were guaranteed success. Billy Cotton's Band was typical of the style that appealed at that time.

In late 1939 a group of musicians, who had been called up, were selected from the ranks to form the RAF Dance Orchestra, known as The Squadronaires. This was hailed as the finest swing band outside America. Led by a Scot, Jimmy Miller from Aberdeen, the players were: Tommy Bradbury, Monty Levy, Jimmy Durrant, Andy McDevitt and Cliff Townshend on sax; Tommy McQuater, Archie Craig and Clinton Ffrench on trumpets; Eric Breeze and George Chisholm on trombones; Ronnie Aldrich, piano; Jock Cummings, drums, Arthur Maden, bass and Sid Colin guitar. The humour was provided by the talented clowning of the Scot, George Chisholm.

Another outstanding band in the RAF called themselves The Skyrockets. The Royal Navy Ordnance Corps had a band called The Blue Rockets and the Royal Navy had The Blue Mariners.

In the early forties Bert Valentine joined the Navy and was posted first to the Far East and then to Bombay. There he was released from service to form the BES Orchestra (British Entertainment for the Services). He played the top favourites from an American dance band, 'I Know Why and So Do You', 'As Time

Prominent figures in the Edinburgh ballroom dance scene, including: back row left, Frank Stewart (Stewart's of Abbeymount); back row second from right, Tony Fusco; front row second from left, Harry Fairley; front row centre, David Sharp (the Silver Slipper); front row, Ena Linton (Eldorado, Excelsior, Paulena's)

Goes By' and 'Tangerine'. The band that had made these and many other numbers popular was the Glen Miller Orchestra.

The American style of music of Glen Miller's Army Air Force Band epitomised the forties, and the band even survived the loss of its leader, Glen Miller, whose plane went missing over the Channel in December 1944. His famous recordings of 'Moonlight Serenade', 'In the Mood' and 'Little Brown Jug' exactly caught the mood of the age and have their devotees even today.

One song which became a wartime hit was discovered by Andy Lothian:

During the War, at the time when Italy ceased hostilities, I was in the RAF, stationed in the toe of Italy. A concert was held to mark the renewal of friendly relations and I heard an Italian airman sing a most beautiful song. Back home in the Dundee Palais I played the song as a waltz and it was an immediate hit – a full six months before it became a national success as the song, 'Come Back to Sorrento'.

War did not stop people dancing. On the contrary, dancing was perceived to be the ideal entertainment for both the uniformed and the civilian. Extra dances were organised to raise funds for the War effort. There were special rates for dancers in uniform. Rules of dress and times of dancing were modified to accommodate the troops in transit. Responding to popular demand, the BBC transmitted dance music every night with Henry Hall from Gleneagles still leading the BBC Dance Orchestra.

There were, of course, a few dissenting voices. In 1941 the Lord's Day Observance Society thundered against Sunday broadcasts. 'It seems appalling that men face to face with the realities of eternity should be regaled with dance music.'

In Scotland, Sunday was a day when dancing in public was generally frowned upon. Saturday night dances always had to finish at midnight. Concerts, on the other hand, were acceptable as they had always been in the period between the Wars as PSAs (Pleasant Sunday Afternoons).

Now, the sudden need to entertain troops and civilians, irrespective of the day of the week, led to confusion and controversy. In 1942 Mr R McEwan formed a Sunday Dance Club in his Sauchiehall Street studio in Glasgow. (Clubs were not bound by the same rules as ballrooms.) The Edinburgh Fountainbridge Palais management found another way round the problem. They held dances on Monday holiday weekends beginning after midnight on Sunday with dancing until 4.00 am.

This may have worked in the big towns but in the smaller towns it was unacceptable. In 1943 the *Scotsman* newspaper reported that Peterhead Sunday Entertainments would hold no Sunday dances in future.

Big bands continued to tour Scotland and huge crowds came to listen to them. In 1940 Joe Loss and his band played to 10,000 dancers in the Glasgow Playhouse in the course of just one week. Louis Freeman had recently taken over the management of this ballroom and established a strong connection with Joe Loss who came to Glasgow regularly. Other famous visiting bands of the time were: Nat Gonella, Herman Darewski, George Scott Wood, Oscar Rabin, Maurice Winnock and George Elrick.

New faces appeared amongst the management of Scotland's ballrooms as men were called up or volunteered for war service. Mr Delworth of the Edinburgh Havanna Club joined the army, Alan Fairley left the Locarno Club for the RASC and Alex Warren joined the RASC in Wales, thereafter serving mainly in East Africa.

It was a time of sad losses too. Teddy Joyce, the band leader, became suddenly ill in Glasgow and died in hospital of cerebro-spinal fever; the death was announced of Mr R Fyfe of the F & F Palais and lessee of the Rothesay Winter Gardens; and in May '41 there was a report of the death of Mr J W Fraser who had been referred to invariably as 'the genial manager of the Marine Gardens'.

Billy MacGregor recalled:

It was hard work during the War. The Gaybirds Band worked at Hillingdon on the fuselages of bombers during the day. We were up at 6.00 am, started at 7.45 am and worked till 8.00 pm. From there we took a tram to Barrowland, working in the ballroom from 9.00 pm to 2.30 am. I remember we often fell asleep waiting for a tram to take us home for a few hours' rest.

Billy MacGregor, the irrepressible leader of The Gaybirds at Barrowland

Everybody had to carry a gas mask at that time. Often the ballroom lights went out during the air-raids. Our boss had anticipated this and had bought fifty or sixty car batteries which he wired up to provide emergency lighting. Later we had a small secondary ballroom called 'Geordie's Ballroom' but it was always candle-lit.

When America came into the War there may have been a feeling of relief in some quarters but for the ballrooms the influx of American soldiers spelled trouble. Andy Lothian had left the Dundee Palais to serve in the Middle East for four years. On his return, he was surprised to find that wartime had affected the atmosphere in the ballroom. It wasn't just the different styles of dancing introduced by the American troops. There was a more subtle difference. He said:

I was aware that there wasn't so much grace in the ballroom. There were a lot of visiting soldiers, sailors and airmen and I had to keep a close eye on some of the lads. In 1940, Polish submarines docked in Dundee and the influx of Polish and American sailors and soldiers caused a lot of resentment amongst the local lads. These visitors wore flashy uniforms and often as not had a packet of nylon stockings in their pockets or a packet of cigarettes, which impressed the girls used to British wartime rationing.

One night it became obvious that there was going to be trouble. The visitors had caught on to the idea of a double novelty dance in which anyone could take over from either dancer by tapping him or her on the shoulder. There was only one thing to do. I stopped the band, gave a roll on the drums and announced that we were going to cool everything down by playing the National Anthem. Everyone had to stand to attention and sing and by the time we finished, tempers were restored.

There was a saying at that time about Americans. British lads complained they were 'over-dressed, over-sexed and over here!'. Billy MacGregor found that the answer to the trouble in Glasgow was to concentrate the American lads in one ballroom:

The American troops could, and sometimes did, cause a lot of trouble in the city because they would flash around nylons, cigarettes and bubble-gum – things that the local lads couldn't compete with. However, it pleased everyone in Glasgow when it worked out that the Yanks went to the Locarno to dance.

Besides scuffles with the Allies, the ballrooms had other unusual problems connected with the War. There was a story of a strange series of events at the Fountainbridge Palais. During the War a young couple met and fell in love. Regular dancers, they decided to ask if they could be married in the ballroom. It was arranged that they could hold the ceremony in front of the bandstand one evening, which they did, following up the ceremony with their favourite dance.

Very shortly afterwards, the young man was called up and, sadly, he was killed in action a few weeks later. The young widow came back to the ballroom to make one last request. She asked permission to scatter her husband's ashes on the ball-room floor. This story may well be apocryphal as there is a similar story connected with a ballroom in Dundee. It does serve to illustrate the kind of myths that attached themselves to wartime ballrooms.

Capacity attendances were reported now in all the dance halls and even after-noon sessions were packed with service men and women on leave along with war workers taking time off between shifts. The dancing sessions were extended to keep up with the demand. The Plaza in Glasgow celebrated its nineteenth birth-day with late sessions almost every evening until 1.00 am. The Albert still kept a self-imposed curfew of 11.00 pm as blackout conditions and lack of transport made journeys home hazardous.

Inevitably, in all ballrooms there were cancellations of events as organisers and participants were liable to be called away; blackout and petrol restrictions made travelling difficult; and rationing affected catering. The Glasgow Plaza was forced to cancel the annual children's party for December 1940 'owing to war conditions' and it was announced that the 'Scottish' championships, run by the *Daily Record*, would be suspended meantime. With great ingenuity, the ball-room managers found alternatives for the thousands of keen dancers. Despite the hazards, the *Dancing Times* of 1941 reported that Glasgow was experiencing its biggest dance boom in many years.

The Palais crowds were always happy to try out new dances. In late 1940 a pre-miere was held for troops in the Paramount Theatre, Glasgow, to launch a new party dance. 'The Anderson Stoop' was devised by John Warren of the Albert, and the music was by George Elrick. (The Anderson shelters were the primitive shel-ters built in back gardens to protect the population from the bombing raids.) The launch of the dance was followed by a first public ballroom demonstration at the Albert when George Elrick himself was in charge of the music. It was reported that 'the dance is a mild skit on the Anderson shelter in quickstep tempo'.

Glasgow set up a Glasgow Ballroom League. It was sponsored by seven city ballrooms. Each ballroom nominated two couples and two reserve couples to dance in the seven ballrooms in turn over a period of seven weeks. The winners would be judged by public applause and silver cups presented to the winning team. The opening contest took place in the Albert in May 1941.

There were also the SDTA Amateur Ballroom Tests held in Diamond's Academy. There were fifty entrants in 1942, and oddly enough, despite the call up, 75 per cent of them were men. Perhaps winning medals was some kind of consolation in wartime.

One form of dancing did suffer a set-back during the early forties. Over the last decade there had sprung up a multitude of dance schools for children. The teachers were inclined to teach more balletic or cabaret dances which their

A group of dancers at Paulena's. Once the Edinburgh Locarno, it was renamed when it was taken over by Paul Collins and Ena Linton

pupils presented to proud parents at end-of-term dance displays. In these displays the children were usually elaborately dressed as 'little Dutch girls' or 'toy soldiers' or the like. Now, in the early forties, owing to war conditions almost all schools of dancing abandoned children's displays. The need for clothing coupons made the supply of costumes difficult and, in any case, many children were being evacuated from the cities.

Despite the influence of American soldiers with their swing style, there was still a strong force towards conformity. Victor Sylvester, the master of strict tempo, founded the BBC Dancing Club in 1941 in which he conducted the orchestra and gave dancing tuition over the radio. These programmes were broadcast worldwide and commanded enormous followings.

There was a large number of Charity Balls during wartime. The Glasgow Plaza raised £1,800 from one ball in 1942 to support Churchill's Aid to Russia Fund.

As time passed and war restrictions became more stringent, all late night sessions had to stop and there was a general close down at 10.45 pm. The only exceptions were the Friday nights at the Glasgow Plaza, and even there, the management announced reluctantly that instead of the usual required formal wear, dress would be optional until further notice. This winter of 1942, the Plaza celebrated its twentieth anniversary and managed to cling to the special 1.00 am close 'while transport permits'.

Rival ballrooms competed for customers with, for example, free Waltz lessons at the New Locarno and free Rumba lessons at the Astoria. Visits from the big bands attracted dancers to the Playhouse where they danced that year to the music of Joe Loss, Nat Gonella, George Scott Wood, Herman Darewski, Maurice Winnock, Carroll Gibbons, Felix Mendelssohn, Lew Stone, Oscar Rabin and George Elrick. Henry Hall played there for two weeks – the first time he had played a full-time engagement in a city ballroom in Scotland. Joe Loss was returning for a fifth time when severe weather in Holland and France delayed him for a week and the gap was filled by Ronnie Munro and his band. At one spectacular Sunday show that season, the American Air Force Band played to an audience of over 4,000. Queues formed daily outside the Plaza and the season marked the 91st anniversary of Diamond's Dancing Academy in Gorbals Street.

Barrowland was so successful that, in 1948, it was expanded, increasing the floor space by half. Although dancers continued to flock in, Billy MacGregor was concerned. He was always unhappy to see so many young girls sitting at the side of the floor as wallflowers while young men showed no inclination to dance with them. After much thought, he finally came up with his idea of Register Dancing.

On admission, each girl was given a book of five numbered cards. The girls could choose partners for five dances giving each partner one of the cards. The boys were eager to collect cards because with them they became eligible for a prize draw.

As a result of this ingenious scheme, there were very few wallflowers between 9.00 pm and 10.30 pm when Register Dancing was in operation. Other ballrooms tried the scheme but it seemed to do best in Barrowland where it continued for many years.

The quality of dancing in Barrowland was said to be the best in the world. Top bands that visited there in the forties included Roy Fox, Henry Hall, Teddy Joyce, Billy Ternant and Jack Hylton. During the War, when other ballrooms banned Jitterbugging because of the physical danger to other dancers, Billy Macgregor set aside space for it and called it Jitterbug Alley. A film featuring Jitterbugging at its best was made there for the Forces.

Such was the dance craze in Glasgow that it was decided to hold open air dancing in Kelvingrove Park. The Corporation Parks Department paid £700 for a sectional dance floor, 100 feet by 800 feet and the venture proved highly successful.

It is difficult for an outsider to appreciate the importance of dance in Glasgow during the thirties and forties. Cliff Hanley recalled how it was:

At the weekends practically every place in Glasgow that had a floor was a dance hall – Masonic halls, Corporation Burgh halls, even church halls. The United Free Church minister once agreed reluctantly to hold a dance. At a certain point in the evening he appeared on the dance floor and announced 'There will be no "hooching"'. [Hooching was the high pitched squeal that normally accompanies the high points in a Highland dance but perhaps the dancers had included an Eightsome Reel in the programme.]

They even had 'Clabbers' in the back courts in the days of the depression. A couple of fellows who could play the fiddle and the accordion would just set it up in the warm weather and people would come and dance in the back courts behind the tenements. My brother used to go to the Drill Hall in Springboig (East end of Glasgow) on a Saturday night. There you paid twopence for the cloakroom and sixpence for entry. A lot of the boys would dodge the cloakroom fee by stuffing their coats behind the rows of stacked chairs. As the evening wore on and the crowds came in, more of the chairs were unstacked revealing the coats. The coats were flung into the middle of the floor and lay there until the red-faced owners went and picked them up and paid their twopence.

From time to time the bouncer would drag some very embarrassed girl into the middle of the floor announcing, 'This wumman has peyed her tanner. She must be danced!'

It is true that a girl could spend her tanner and not be danced all evening. Often a very good-looking lassie would have a frumpish friend attached to her. Boys would often come in twos giving rise to the old Glasgow saying, 'I don't fancy the one you're gettin', Jimmy'.

But in Glasgow, a lot of folk didn't go for romance. They went for dancing. If romance did blossom, the boy might offer to see his partner home but much depended on where the girl lived. 'Where do you live, hen? Coatbridge? It's no' a lumber you want, it's a pen-pal.' [A lumber was a boy-friend.]

During the War, the Americans had their club at the Grand Hotel, Charing Cross, in Glasgow. The Locarno was just along the street so most of them went there. Crooning had come into vogue in the thirties with Rudi Vallee and Bing Crosby. Now, in wartime, Glasgow was full of crooners. It was a great singing city. The Locarno had crooning competitions when young hopefuls would sing into the mike songs like 'The White Cliffs of Dover' and 'I'll be Seeing You'.

With so many ballrooms in the city it was always possible for numbers to drop in one in favour of another. The Tower ballroom was small and enjoyed a reputation for good music and tough clientele. Cliff Hanley remembered, 'One night there were only two couples in and the band leader announced a Paul Jones. That finished with a big punch-up.'

During the war, in fact during the thirties and forties, you wore dance shoes. Boys had black patent leather with fine leather soles. The girls would carry their shoes in their shoulder bags (silver strappy shoes with high heels) but the boys always carried theirs in brown paper bags. On busy nights a queue would form with all the boys carrying brown paper bags under their arms.

In the season 1944 to 1945 the Education Authorities were becoming concerned about the effect of dancing fever on their young pupils. There had been a move to introduce basic country and ballroom dancing to the school curriculum but this had met with opposition from dancing teachers who feared the effect that 'unqualified teachers of dance' might have on the pupils – not to mention their own loss of revenue if dancing was included in normal school work.

In schools, the practice continued of 'drilling' the basic steps of the Waltz, Fox Trot and Quick Step in the weeks leading up to the Christmas Dance. Despite or because of this, pupils left school and took to the dance halls and evening classes to bring themselves up to standard. Lanarkshire Education Authority were perturbed when it was revealed that out of 5,000 girls attending their classes, only 147 opted for cooking while 940 chose to go to classes for ballroom and country dancing. The dilemma was unresolved. Nothing and nobody could stop the dancing.

There was every reason to dance in 1945 when the end of the War brought victory celebration events all over Scotland. In Glasgow, several public parks had open air dancing and 500 seamen held a dance in the Merchant Navy Reserve Pool Hostel. The Playhouse held a Cinema Victory Ball in fancy dress with a personal appearance by Eric Portman, the film star, as an extra attraction. That evening 1,300 dancers danced to the music of Oscar Rabin.

The end of the War brought some relaxations. The Ayr Pavilion was released by the army for dancing. Sadly, the Marine Gardens in Portobello was never to open again as a ballroom. Another disappointment came when it was announced that the Scottish National Dancing Championships would no longer be run by the *Daily Record* because of the difficulties arising from the shortage of newsprint. However, this problem was resolved when the SDTA took over the competition with Alex Warren in charge. Heats started in November with the finals in March 1946. The West of Scotland Championships also resumed in September in the Albert with the indefatigable Alex Warren in control.

After the war, a few service bands like the Squadronaires and the Skyrockets decided to stay together but they were faced with an unexpected problem – where to play. During the war, the usual venues such as big hotels, clubs and restaurants had been forced to make do with smaller bands. They had discovered that dancers were perfectly happy with this arrangement and managements were therefore reluctant to return to the more expensive big bands.

The Sky Rockets gave up the idea of being a dance band altogether when they were appointed as the pit orchestra at the London Palladium. Others, like the Squadronaires, were forced to take to the road on exhausting one-night stands in ballrooms across the country. The only band that appeared to buck the trend was the new Ted Heath Band formed in 1945.

Some big bands gave up completely and 1946 saw the disbandment of many famous name bands: Benny Goodman, Woody Herman, Harry James, Tommy Dorsey, Les Brown, Jack Teagarden and Benny Carter. The awful truth was that the era of the big bands was coming to an end.

1946 seemed to mark a sharp increase in the number of competitions. A returning triumphant army may have felt the need to prove themselves in peacetime competition; or, possibly, the ballroom managements may have seized on the opportunity to restore the excitement of competition to jaded palates. Whatever the reason, there was a flurry of championships in Scotland.

The Edinburgh and East of Scotland Ballroom Proprietors' Association held twelve championships and the Annual Holiday Dancing Contest resumed in Aberdeen after a gap of seven years. There was also the Aberdeen Challenge Trophy limited to Scottish professional couples and won by Alex and Peggy Provan.

The 13th Scottish National Dancing Championships, which were open to amateurs, attracted huge numbers, involving sixty ballrooms with the heats and culminating in the finals in March 1938 in Glasgow's St Andrew's Halls. These were, perhaps the most prestigious championships and the winners were presented with the *Daily Record* Challenge Trophy.

The West of Scotland Amateur Ballroom Championships went ahead at the Albert as usual. As well as running the Albert and promoting ballroom dancing at every opportunity, Alex Warren became a Councillor of the City of Glasgow, a move which began almost three decades of public service.

In Edinburgh, the North British Ballrooms Association held the Scottish Professional Championships at the Fountainbridge Palais and grandly advertised them as 'open to the world'. The finals took place on 29 August during the Edinburgh Festival. Some 3,000 dancers attended and 25 couples competed for the top cash prizes of £150. The winners were Victor Barrett with Doreen Freeman, and Len Scrivener with Nellie Duggan.

Barrowland hit the headlines again when it was selected as a location for a major film: 1,000 dancers swung to the music of Billy MacGregor and his Gaybirds in the film *Floodtide*.

1948 brought good news and bad news for ballroom dancing. The *Dancing Times* reported that 'the War Office have now completely de-requisitioned ballrooms'. On the other hand, bad weather resulted in the worst-ever season for open air dancing at Kelvingrove Park in Glasgow. There were hardly two dry

Bert Valentine and Band on the road

nights in succession during the season, with the exception of a fortnight in July when it was too cold even though it was dry.

To add to the miseries, a huge fire destroyed the F & F Palais which had first opened in 1922. 300 dancers were evacuated as the fire took hold.

Dancing at this time tended to be a douce affair as servicemen returned to their wives and families. The wild Jitterbug was seen less often and had been softened into Jive. Bert Valentine, back from the War, first backed the singer David Hughes, and did a season in Dunoon with Andy Stewart. In 1946 he moved to Fife where the most popular band, the Hill family, Roland, Bob and George, played in the Raith Ballroom in Kirkcaldy. Finally, in 1948 he joined Alex McLaughlan and his resident band at Macdonald's Ballroom in Fettes Row:

> Mr Macdonald was known as the King of Old Time Dancing. He was always dressed in immaculate evening dress but he looked as if he carried the world's troubles on his shoulders. To begin with I was paid £2.50 a night but eventually I was appointed band leader and paid more. We played every kind of Old Time dance and did the occasional broadcast.
>
> Mr Macdonald was a stickler for etiquette. Nobody danced till he and his wife graced the floor first.

As a most particular compliment, Mr Macdonald created 'The Valentine Waltz' in Bert's honour and Bert wrote the music for it.

This was the year the young Princess Elizabeth and her new husband, the Duke of Edinburgh, visited Scotland. The *Dancing Times* reported:

At the reception and dance held in the Assembly Rooms, Edinburgh, and attended by Princess Elizabeth and the Duke of Edinburgh, an outstanding item on the programme was the dancing of the new 'Duke and Duchess of Edinburgh Reel'. Both Royal guests watched the performance closely, the Duke looking a little puzzled.

There was another dancing landmark this year when Victor Sylvester founded 'Television Dancing Club'. For the first time, fans could see the master demonstrate the dances instead of listening to his voice describing them. This was also the beginning of the fixed image of a 'ballroom dancer' in the frothy layers of sequined net.

Fashions had changed throughout the War years as clothes rationing limited choices. The end of the War brought longer dresses, the 'New Look', and more daring styles. Some young men were attracted to what was known as the 'Spiv' style but it failed to find favour with the establishment.

The *Melody Maker* reported in February 1949:

> The BBC is evidently allergic to spivs. They recently imposed a ban on 'Fiddler's Serenade', a natty song published by Buchanan-Dunlop . . . The lyric, they said, glamorised the spiv.
>
> It went like this: 'He's a flashy kind of guy, wears a rainbow-coloured tie, and he fiddles, fiddles, fiddles all day long. So beware, so beware if you meet him in the Strand or Leicester Square. He's the talk of London Town and he'll do you up or down, so beware . . .'
>
> The song has now been amended thus: 'If you only know the sign, brother you'll be doing fine, it's a fiddle, fiddle, fiddle all day long; So beware, so beware, you can bet your life it happens everywhere. If you know just what to do, then you'll never have to queue, so beware . . .'[1]

Melody Maker could see no improvement but the BBC declared itself satisfied and the song got its first airing that month.

Vocalists continued to be a major attraction in the ballrooms. From America, through the popular films of the day, through radio and records, came a galaxy of singers in great demand: Dick Haynes, Peggy Lee, Perry Como, Doris Day, Ella Fitzgerald, Frank Sinatra and Jo Stafford. Britain had Anne Shelton, Vera Lynn and Alma Cogan. In the ballrooms, even the smallest dance band had its vocalist. A favourite in Edinburgh was Jackie McFarlane, the jazz singer with the gritty voice nicknamed 'Mr 5 by 5'.

In 1949 ballroom dancing was still a profitable concern and Glasgow Corporation seriously considered holding dances in public halls to make up deficits in their budget. The Scottish Industries Exhibition brought many visitors to the city and the ballrooms were all busy.

Billy MacGregor recalled:

> In Barrowland we had nine full-time bouncers on the dance floor for up to 3,000 dancers. There were more bouncers on the doors so fights were soon stopped. At that time there were seven theatres in Glasgow and the big bands topped the bill there and then moved on to the ballrooms for Friday night sessions ending at 3 am.

It was a good time to work in the ballrooms in Glasgow. Each of the big thirteen ballrooms took it in turn to hold a staff dance after the normal session. Then all the other bands came on for half hour sessions and these were great occasions.

It was great but change was in the air. On the horizon were such radical changes that dance and ballrooms would never be the same.

CHAPTER EIGHT

From Couples to Individuals

༄ ༄

1950 to the Present

In the early years of the fifties it appeared on the surface as if nothing would change. Victor Sylvester's fortnightly 'Television Dancing Club' was still advocating the old style. British teachers were justly proud of their 'English Style', which had spread abroad, where it was known as 'the Standard Dances' in Europe and 'International Style' in North America and Australia.

The main dances for competition purposes were still the Waltz, Fox Trot, Tango and Quickstep.

Old Time dancing was achieving an amazing return to popularity. Old Time Dance clubs sprang up in their thousands after the war. Unfortunately, the name, sometimes transmuted to 'Olde Tyme' was not calculated to appeal to the young. It did appeal to families who enjoyed social dancing. The main attraction came from the fact that all dancers on the floor performed the same steps at the same time. At that time, the Official Board of Ballroom Dancing had nine members who specialised in teaching this form of dancing and each year there were competitions to discover the best new sequence dance. However, the old standards remained top favourites: Waltz, Veleta, Boston Two-step, Military Two-step and Lancers.

Television Dancing Club was also, to an extent, frozen in aspic. The cream of professional dancers gave demonstrations of steps and took part in competitions. The dancers wore what was almost a uniform. Ladies appeared in skirts of tulle with as many as a hundred yards of material designed to flow with the movement of the dance. With tiny bodices held up by narrow straps, the dresses, often decorated with thousands of sequins, looked like glittering puff balls. It became a television cliché that the compere would announce 'Beryl's dress has three thousand sequins and she sewed them all on herself.'

Televised lessons for children were given by Phyllis Haylor and Victor Barrett from
Limegrove Studios in November 1950 (*courtesy of* The Dancing Times)

The men were equally uniform, wearing a version of evening dress that
sported long swallow tails which came well below the knee and which were also
designed to move with the dance. Lapels were often anchored by a cord to
prevent them from opening out during rapid turns.

Since the end of the war, competition had grown to such an extent that one
writer described it as 'almost a disease'.[1] The Amateur and the Professional
Championships at Blackpool Winter Gardens remained the best organised
events, and the British Championship titles from Blackpool were more coveted
than the Star World Championship titles from London. By the end of the decade
there were about 300 championships on offer throughout Britain organised by
big commercial enterprises.

In the midst of all this conformity, there was a new influence which started in
the late forties and began to boom in the early fifties – Latin American dancing.
Following the success of the Rumba came the Samba.

The Samba in Brazil is a generic term indicating dances of African origin.
There are different kinds of Samba from different regions but these rural Sambas
share a common factor. They are accompanied by percussion instruments only.
The rural Sambas were group dances but the ballroom Samba was a couple
dance which had links to the Brazilian Maxixe and the African Lundu. The
dancing thousands didn't waste time studying the complicated background.

What they enjoyed about the dance was the rhythm, known everywhere as the Latin rhythm or Latin American. Latin American bands like those led by Edmundo Ros and Roberto Inglese became hugely popular.

A new style of Cuban dance came with new style Cuban music which in turn had been influenced by American jazz and swing. The important difference was the accentuation of the off-beats. In the early fifties another dance, the Mambo, had one beat in every bar on which no step was taken. British schools of dance incorporated Mambo music with a new style of Rumba to produce a dance that was very different from the version danced in America and on the Continent.

In America the music was developed into three rhythms: single mambo, double mambo and triple mambo. Triple mambo with five beats to a bar led to another new dance in Britain called the Cha-Cha. Latin American dancing was easily absorbed into the ballrooms which had, after all, coped with many new dances in the past.

The ballrooms were still doing very good business. Glasgow was still a city of dancers. Cliff Hanley said, 'Growing up in a city where standards were universally high made you critical even of dancers in movies. They couldn't do a reverse turn or a fish tail or a telemark!'

A group of Championship judges in 1955. Left to right: Marie Mitchell, Nan Dalgleish, Anne Warren, Peggy Provan, Ena Linton

A youthful Farquhar MacRae (nicknamed 'Flash' because of his immaculate appearance) took over management of the Berkeley Ballroom in Glasgow in the early fifties

Easy dances were scorned by the Glasgow regulars. The simple Empress Tango was strictly for grannies.

Ballroom dancing is a telepathic operation. The girl has to know a fraction of a second before the man leads where he is leading her. Good dancing partners who could 'dance as one' were always in demand.

At this time, the ever popular Glasgow Plaza had a new manager, Adam Sharp, who came from Aberdeen in 1952. Adam brought one innovation to the Plaza when he trained a Plaza formation dance team called the Starlight Formation. They always danced to 'star' music like, for example, 'When You Wish Upon a Star', and, as a final touch of showbiz, at the end of the sequence all the ballroom lights were put out and the music changed to 'Dancing in the Dark'. Audiences were amazed when the ladies' dresses lit up with coloured lights which were attached to their skirts.

Formation dancing was another variant of the English Style which had been made popular by the 'Television Dancing Club'. A number of couples (usually eight) would make intricate patterns on the floor, always keeping to the same steps and the same movements. It required strict discipline and strict tempo and was, of course, ideal televisual material where a camera could rise above the floor and display the patterns most effectively.

It was, however, a demanding kind of dancing and although television audiences could watch regular demonstrations and competitions, it was never a popular form. Franks claimed that by the end of the fifties there were not more than 50 formation teams throughout the country and the majority of those sprang up after television began to make its demands for them.[2]

In his book *Social Dance*, Franks was equally dismissive of competition dancing and provided figures to support his view:

> A mistaken impression has sprung up as to the extent and strength of this kind of dancing. In fact it is very small. Registered with the Official Board are fewer than 3,000 dancers, 1,500 couples. There are probably not as many as 5,000 dancers who regularly enter competitions in Britain. It provides a spectacle but is only a fringe activity. The vast bulk of people who go dancing do not wish to learn the style. It is too difficult and it requires too much floor space.

This was a rather simplistic view which failed to take into consideration that this kind of dancing had become a spectator sport attracting huge, partisan audiences. You might just as well count the number of professional football players in the country and claim that this was a fringe activity.

Paul Collins with his formation dance team in Green's Playhouse in Glasgow

East of Scotland Old Time Dancing Championship, Princes Street Gardens, Edinburgh 16 August 1958 (*Courtesy of the Edinburgh* Evening News)

A ballroom that bucked the trend was the Cavendish in Edinburgh. With Tim Wright in charge, this ballroom was one of the very few to specialise in Scottish Country Dancing. During the early fifties every Tuesday and Thursday evening was given over to this form of dance. They were the first band to be televised with a group of Scottish Country Dancers in the fifties.

Scottish Country Dancing had never been part of the mainstream of ballroom dancing although the occasional eightsome reel might be included in a club dance. This is not to say that it had died out. On the contrary. Country Dancing has always been an integral part of Clan Gatherings and Highland Balls. To an extent it was the preferred dancing for country people and also for the nobility in Scotland. The supreme band leader in Scotland for Scottish Country Dancing was Jimmy Shand, whose name became synonymous with the best of Scottish music.

Tim Wright and his band at the Cavendish in Edinburgh

In the fifties the main ballrooms employed a singer with the dance band. Billy MacGregor always had two or three in Barrowland. He remembered how he made one discovery:

> I was looking for another singer and there were always girls hanging about the bandstand. One Sunday afternoon four members of the band came in and we auditioned thirty girls. Some of them couldn't even sing in tune and I was fed up. Then young Helen Thomson came on and sang 'I Love Paris'. She had a good voice but she was shy and stiff. I decided to take her on. We rehearsed every day for eight weeks . She learned a new song every week and eventually she became very good so I put her on.

In 1958 Lou Preger had a competition for singers. Helen entered the Scottish heat which was held at the Albert. Helen won the heat. With the help of Alex Warren who helped with her fare she went to London for the finals, where she came fourth. She decided to stay on in London with encouragement from George Elrick. Helen was doing quite well in the night clubs, but George suggested that she would do better if she changed her name. The story is told that a bottle of brandy on his table gave him inspiration and she became Lena Martell. She had a chequered career but is still singing.

The major change in ballroom dancing came in the mid-fifties. It came, once again, from America where Charlie Parker and Dizzie Gillespie were turning their music into complicated harmonic progressions they called Be-bop. This kind of improvisation was so free and unpredictable that it was impossible to dance to. Fans were reduced to standing round the band and moving their bodies in time to the beat.

Sid Colin described what happened next:

> The times were ripe for change . . . it came in 1955 with Bill Haley, a chubby American with a slick of damp hair who played country guitar and led a six-piece band which he called his Comets. The music was crude – the melody nursery rhyme simple . . . they called it Rock and Roll. 'One two three o'clock four o'clock rock, five six seven o'clock, eight o'clock rock – nine ten eleven o'clock, twelve o'clock rock, we're gonna rock! around! the clock! tonight! . . .' The musicians were appalled but Bill Haley's rock and roll sold a zillion records.[3]

The man who actually coined the term, 'rock and roll' was Alan Freed, a classical disc jockey from Cleveland, Ohio. He was fascinated by the way the kids moved when they danced. Singers like Elvis Presley, Fabian and Frankie Avalon encouraged the teenage rebellion. In Britain, Tommy Steele and Cliff Richard produced their own form of rock and roll.

What happened next was, according to Rust, 'more in the nature of a mass phenomenon for teenage dancers'.[4] Post-war babies had grown into their teens in a world of welfare state and full employment. At packed cinemas, the film, *Rock Around the Clock* had them out of their seats and dancing in the aisles. They had found the identity they were looking for. Teenage power had begun.

The beat was new, the dance was wild and acrobatic. The style was flexible and impossible to standardise. Quirey described it as

> more overtly sexual. The count was a simple one, one, two, one, two, in line with the pounding beat, and there was no rule about which partner should use which foot at any one time. It was hard to tell who was leading; it could be either the man or the girl and sometimes it didn't matter at all; but it was still alright to throw your partner around in a manner that simulated the most athletic kind of sex. The girl would throw her legs around the man's waist, lean back and open her legs, and the two would swirl around each other (or over, or under), fingertips clutched and arms outstretched.[5]

Along with the style of the dance came the style of the dress. Girls wore their hair tied back in pony tails and had ballet-length circular skirts with layers of net underskirts frothing underneath. They wore either flat shoes and white socks or stiletto heels and nylons, and they used bright red lipstick. The boys were equally flamboyant with long 'teddy boy' jackets, drain-pipe trousers, greased hair, luminous socks, boot-lace ties and thick crêpe soled shoes or shoes with pointed toes called 'winklepickers'.

In the late fifties there was another blow for teenage independence. Lonnie Donegan introduced Skiffle music. With a string bass, a drum, a guitar and a singing voice, he produced a series of hits and young people all over the country began to copy him and make their own music, using whatever instruments came to hand, from a tea chest and broom handle to a washboard.

1958 brought a double loss to dancing at Barrowland. Mrs McIver died leaving her sons, Sam and John, to carry on the business; and on 19 August, Barrowland was burned to the ground. Plans to rebuild began immediately.

The newly built Barrowland Ballroom was even bigger than before and it opened its doors on Christmas Eve 1960. Billy MacGregor and the Gaybirds were back and remained there until 1969. The open policy of the ballroom was made clear from the start. The opening night was a Teenage Jamboree and on the following Thursday there was 'a Teen Plus Night (for Mammy, Daddy, yes and Granny!)'

Once again, the huge crowds rolled in, with up to 9,000 dancers every week. An extra candle-lit dancing area called Geordie's Byre was opened in 1961. Throughout the sixties Barrowland made a feature of bringing in the best rock stars of the day. When Gene Vincent, the rock and roll singer, starred in 1961, he had to be smuggled out through a back door at the end of the evening, leaving angry scenes in the street as thwarted fans realised what had happened.

February 1962 saw the arrival in Barrowland of a new dance called the Twist. Another American import, it had been introduced by Chubby Checker along with the music, 'Let's Twist Again'. The Twist was described as a dance where you tried to stub out a cigarette with your toe while you dried your back with a towel.

It introduced an era where a partner was no longer strictly necessary. In some ways it was a ballroom proprietor's dream because it took up so little space. Rust believed the dance was a development from the exaggerated arm and hip movements of singers of rock music. It was certainly the first dance to benefit from heavy media marketing.

The big firms of Rank, Mecca and Columbia were the first to capitalise on the large, relatively affluent, teenage market. The advent of cheap, unbreakable and easily portable records supplied the tools of the trade. The first long-playing records appeared. LPs were issued in America in 1949. Decca issued the first LPs in Britain in June 1950, followed by EMI in Autumn 1952 with LPs and 45s. ('45' referred to the number of revolutions per minute – the speed of the records). Because 45s were small, plastic and cheap, teenagers bought them in their millions.

Blanket publicity across Britain for the Twist included dresses, hair styles and shoes. A book, *Dance the Twist* by Norman Dwyer, sold out its first print of 125,000 in ten days.

One of the benefits of this dance was that, since it was individual, there was no need to accommodate a partner. It could be varied according to age and energy levels. In 1963 it was even accorded Royal approval when it was included at the Queen's Dance at Windsor Castle to celebrate the engagement of Princess Alexandra.

The dance that followed the Twist was linked with the 'Mod' cult. It challenged the rock and roll of the 'Rockers' and was called the Shake. This was so minimal it was hardly a dance at all. Rust describes it as a dance where 'the feet hardly

Ten year old Valerie dancing with her grandfather, John Warren, on Christmas Eve 1953 at a re-opening Gala following a fire at the Albert. The band wore comedy firemen's helmets and led off their quickstep selection with 'I'm Sitting On Top of the World' - the number they played as the dancers filed out from beneath the burning roof three weeks earlier

moved but legs vibrated and hands gesticulated, the shoulders swung and the head quivered and twitched'.[6]

A Jamaican influence arrived with the Blue Beat, Ska or Ska Blues. In 1964 a Jamaican teenager called Millie Small produced a Ska version of an American pop song called 'Lollipop' which featured on the television programme Top of the Pops and brought a wave of enthusiasm across the country for what was renamed the Blue Beat Sound. Rust sums it up: 'They all dance the Blue Beat stiff at the knees, throw arms everywhere, hips to the side, four beats at a time. There is a fast, monotonous rhythm and a very heavily accented off-beat.'[7]

By 1969 there were at least 25,000 Beat Groups in Britain. The young had taken over and were making their own music. The Mersey Sound with the Beatles and the Rolling Stones was drawing in huge hysterical crowds of young people. The ballrooms were forced to take a stand or to change their image totally.

The crowds were still there but there was a massive split developing. It was a division by age. The young scorned the dances of their parents and their parents were unwilling or unable to do the new dances. Some ballrooms, like

Barrowland, managed to find a way to accommodate both styles but many refused to allow the new dances and continued to play as before to an aging dancing population.

The home of good ballroom dancing, the Albert, continued to hold a special place in the hearts of keen dancers in Glasgow. Dances were always strictly to correct tempo and good manners were always insisted upon. From 1959 to the early sixties John Warren produced dance records under the Pye label using a dozen of the best session musicians in London. They included George Chisholm, trombone; Red Price, tenor sax; Martin Slavin, jazz vibist; Joe Mudele, jazz bassist; Marie Goosens, harpist, and Bernard Marshin, violinist. The records, which all began with the sound of an unaccompanied metronome, were released as 'The John Warren Strictempo Orchestra'. The changing fashions in dancing finally closed the ballroom and it was sold in 1965. A more final and dramatic end came in 1974 when the building was destroyed by fire.

It was far from the end of ballroom dance interests for Alex Warren. During the past twenty years he had suffered the loss of his mother, Annie, in 1947; his father, John, in 1957; his wife, Nellie, in 1963, and his brother, John, in 1969. He had followed a distinguished path in Public Service as City Magistrate, Police Judge, JP and Deputy Lieutenant. He continued as patron, adjudicator and organiser of ballroom dancing events. He married again in 1966. During the

1962 and Valerie Anne Brown at the Albert is twisting the Madison, which John Warren hoped to take to the Top Twenty programme on television as the latest dance craze.
This was at a time when Alex Warren caused an uproar by pointing out that Victor Sylvester was not qualified to judge Latin-American competitions as he had no personal qualifications in Latin-American dancing

following decade he was to be showered with awards for a lifetime of service. In 1973 he was presented with the Carl Alan Award for the person who did most for ballroom dancing. Also in 1973 he was invited back to New York to compère the World Dancing Championships in Madison Square Gardens. In 1974 he took his new wife, Jessie, to Buckingham Palace where he was awarded the OBE. His sister Anne died in 1982. Alex Warren died in 1990 – a champion of ballroom dancing in every sense of the word.

The changing styles affected the Fountainbridge Palais in Edinburgh like all the rest. In 1963 Mr Bill Robertson became manager. He struggled to bring in attractions like the popular singer, Sandie Shaw, but the ballroom was in trouble. A stabbing brought in the police one night. The boiler burst and the balcony was declared unsafe. The doors were closed to dancers in the '67 to '68 season and a proud ballroom eventually became a Bingo Hall.

For a while, the Edinburgh Plaza managed to keep a loyal following, but by the mid sixties the main ballroom had to be adapted to the Rock style and a banner over the stage proclaimed 'Pick of the Pops'. It was a token gesture and the management still clung to the older standards of dress and behaviour. The barring of a prospective dancer wearing the latest roll-neck shirt brought newspaper comment. The aggrieved customer complained, 'The management of a public dance hall have no justification for such a restriction in this supposedly enlightened age.' The management responded, 'People should remember it's a dance they're going to, not an apres-ski affair.'[8] It was a brave stand with as much hope of success as Canute.

Dwindling numbers brought the dancing to an end. The Edinburgh *Evening News* published a sad notice on 1 March 1975: 'Take Your Partners – the Last Waltz'.[9] To the music of Bert Valentine's Midway Band, the Plaza closed its doors for the last time.

Joe Smith, the manager since 1947, remembered:

Thursday night's over-25 session was nostalgic and emotional. We had a couple who came back after 26 years for a final dance. A regular couple (he was 72 and she was 70), they danced the Tango just as they did in the ballroom 30 years ago. There were a lot of tears at the end.

The building was finally demolished and a new Safeway superstore built on the site. Safeway displays a plaque commemorating the Plaza and lamp-posts in local streets still carry parking notices referring to the late nights at the Plaza.

In Dundee, the Palais continued until the retiral of Andy Lothian in 1977. He sold it, but before it could be developed the building went up in flames.

There were a few ballroom survivors. In Dundee, the Star Ballroom managed by Bob Barty still operates six nights a week at the time of writing. There are disco classes for children in the afternoons and there is also tuition during the course of the evening sessions.

In the Aberdeen Beach Ballroom the floor has been reduced in size but the

Bob Barty leading the dancers at the Star Ballroom in Dundee

ballroom is still operating for functions and on special occasions, although a fire in late 1993 may delay plans for an expanded programme.

Following the Twist in the seventies came the latest and so far unchallenged newcomer, disco dancing. Victor Sylvester claimed that it had made the biggest impact on the public of any dance since the Charleston. 'The main distinction being that partners do not touch at all. It is very much a solo dance, danced on the spot with the partners facing each other.'[10]

The king of the dance teachers had strong views about disco dancing. 'In my opinion the dancing profession has been very lax in not laying down a few simple figures to act as a guide for those who wish to learn this form of rhythmic movement, which can be danced to Beat music in 4/4 time'.

His simple steps were: 'short step to side with RF; close LF to RF keeping weight on RF; short step to side with LF; close RF to LF keeping weight on LF'. The trouble was that the steps gave no help at all to dancers who could not dance them in the required 'easy, relaxed manner'. Body, arm and hip actions were required and the suggestion in a subsequent 'Teach Yourself' book by the Imperial Society of Teachers of Dancing that 'arm movements often reflect day to day actions, such as serving at tennis, skating, swimming, answering the telephone etc.'[11] would do little to help beginners today. Disco dancing was as much an attitude of mind as a dance and its appeal was mainly to the young.

The Locarno in Glasgow was one ballroom which took to disco in a big way. Renamed Tiffany's it eventually closed to become a casino.

The Glasgow Plaza under the management of Adam Sharp continued to be the home of ballroom dancers until his retirement in 1990. The last of the great ballrooms, it struggled to keep going in an atmosphere of faded glamour. New managements used late night discos and rave parties to subsidise the afternoon and early evening sessions of dancing. Then in 1992 Scottish and Newcastle refurbished the ballroom, and dancing continues.

In Edinburgh, the Cavendish, while not the largest ballroom, has proved to be the most adaptable and enduring, and is still in operation at the time of writing. It has seen many sea changes. On the death of Tim Wright in 1961 it continued under the management of Andy Bathgate. He tried to renew the link with the Scottish Country Dance Society but unfortunately the change in popular tastes made this an economic impossibility. His vision for the 'New Cavendish' was doomed and it was forced to close.

However, this was not the end of the story. In 1972 Unicorn Leisure took over and renamed it Clouds. It became a roller-skating rink and a disco later to be renamed Coasters, with an evening club called the Bermuda Triangle. This last name was perhaps tempting fate, because fire gutted the building in October 1985. Once again it was rebuilt. In time Coasters was re-named the Outer Limits. In 1988 it changed again to Network and developed a bad reputation for violence.

The business was rescued by European Leisure, who decided to reintroduce once a week ballroom dancing and to go back to the old name of the New Cavendish Club. With Tommy Sampson in charge of an 18-piece band the evenings became popular with a limited public. Currently, the owners are considering the possibility of continuing these evenings to cater for the hard core of enthusiasts. Nightly Disco dancing for the over 25s is now prospering.

Finally, as a building but no longer a ballroom, Barrowland is perhaps the biggest survivor. Under the leadership of Billy MacGregor it weathered the sixties with little trouble despite one or two violent episodes of stabbings and a notorious case of murder connected to a mysterious killer nicknamed Bible John. It hosted the only appearance in Scotland of Bill Haley and his Comets in September 1964 and thousands danced to the tune of the day, 'See You later Alligator'. Lulu and the Luvvers, Herman's Hermits, and the Kinks were all popular visitors. By 1968 ballroom sessions were reduced to once a week and this continued when in 1969 Jimmy Phillips took over as a new leader. There was a brief 'Learn to Dance' campaign in 1972, but it was dealt a death blow in 1973 when Barrowland was granted a drink licence. Within a week or two crowds fell away as the law did not permit young people under the age of 21 to attend licensed premises. Dancing came to an end and the ballroom closed. However, it was re-discovered as a major venue for musicians and it continues to attract thousands who come to listen rather than to dance.

There were, of course, teachers who survived the changes and continued to

Warren Brown and his wife, Aileen Turner, winning the Scottish Amateur Modern
Championship in 1968

bridge the gulf by teaching both the standard dances and a version of Rock and
Roll. Reg and Marjorie Harkins were popular in Edinburgh. They had three
schools of dancing, the Edina, the Central School and the Afton. Dancers progressed from one to the other as their dancing improved. In the fifties lessons
cost five shillings for half an hour. The main dances then were the Rumba, the
Samba, Cha-Cha and Jive. Their school finally closed in 1970 as 'demand was
diminishing and new dances didn't need teachers.'

In the nineties there are still dancing schools advertising ballroom dancing
lessons, but the majority concentrate on teaching children. Annual displays tend
to show a variety of styles from ballet to tap with an emphasis on stage work.
Adult ballroom dancers are more likely to go in for medal competitions and there
are still opportunities for those with talent to work their way to the top of the
dancing world. Amongst the successful teachers, few can have the pedigree of

Warren Brown jnr with partner, Rebecca Hannant, in 1993, following in his parents'
footsteps

Warren Brown, son of Anne Warren. The Warren dynasty continues with his son,
who in the fourth generation of this dancing family, has already achieved ballroom dancing success.

Scotland has its dancing stars. One of the best-known Scottish couples, Bill
and Bobby Irvine, dominated the professional circuits and appeared regularly on
television. Bill, who came from Kilsyth, said that Britain, the home of ballroom
dancing, fails to respect it in the way the Germans or the Japanese do today:
'Ballroom dancing is an Art Form. It has definite techniques and requires
tremendous discipline and training. In effect two people are trying to accomplish
the same thing at the same time – trying to dance as one.'

Another Scot achieving tremendous professional success is Donnie Burns and
his partner Gaynor Fairweather, ten times top Latin-American dancers in the
world. A pupil of the late Harry Rollins, Donny first won the World

Bill and Bobby Irvine, top British and International professional dancers who
dominated the championships from the early sixties. Their elegance and style made
them favourites in the 'Come Dancing' programmes on television

Championship in Norway in 1985. Latin-American dancing has become formal-
ised and very athletic. Judges look for choreography and presentation in what
looks increasingly like an elaborate cabaret act.

Donny and Gaynor are amongst the few champions who do not teach dancing,
preferring to concentrate on their own competitive dancing. They live and train
for part of the year in Japan where they are accorded the status of superstars. On
one occasion they filled the Tokyo Dome with 35,000 people for a run of three
nights. A dedicated couple, they admit that their ultimate goal of 'perfection' is
unattainable.

There are those who regret the passing of the dancing boom of the twenties,

124

Donnie Burns and Gaynor Fairweather. Even in the dancing world of superlatives these two are something of a phenomenon. In countries like Japan where ballroom dancing is still a popular pursuit they have achieved cult status reminiscent of the days of Casani and Lennard

thirties and forties, but for them Sid Colin offers sober words of warning: 'It is as well to remember what they were the musical accompaniment to. A lacerating depression, a second World War and the Nazi holocaust.'[12]

Dancing has changed and changed again over the centuries but perhaps some things will never change. It is said that dancing has become a way of displaying yourself, but was that not equally true of the dancers who displayed their dresses in the Grand March in 1600? Young dancers claim that their discos give them a way of expressing freedom from conventional restraint. Was that not the claim of the dancers of the Charleston?

At the time of writing there are a number of places in Scotland where ballroom dancing is practised. The Assembly Rooms in Edinburgh and Kelvin Hall in Glasgow have regular tea dances and there are many small halls and clubs with dancing on several nights each week. At the LRT hall in Annandale Street in Edinburgh, for example, there is sequence dancing five nights a week and freestyle on the sixth night.

The Edinburgh *Evening News* of September 1979 reported on the disco fever in the city. Declaring ballrooms of the past to be austere, and dancing 'rigidly conservative and a prude's paradise' the report concluded that

> the staid, straight-laced school-marms of those days would throw up their hands in horror if they could see us now! At one, two or three o'clock in the morning Edinburgh is alive and swinging.[13]

Such is the short memory of folk history.

In March 1994 the Edinburgh *Evening News* heralded the arrival of a new dance craze called the Doop. The Doop is a modern version of the Charleston! Amongst the dance crazes listed as past history are the Jitterbug of the forties, Rock and Roll of the fifties and the Twist of the sixties. The seventies are credited with Disco, Slamdancing and Headbanging; the eighties with Breakdancing and the Lambada. Rave dancing in the nineties is described as 'adaptable DIY dance-floor routines' ranging from 'a subdued shaking of imaginary maracas to an imitation of someone wired to the National Grid.'

The fact remains that people are still dancing and although they no longer call their floors ballrooms, the dancers are still having a ball.

EPILOGUE

The End of an Era?

∽ ∾

The heyday of ballroom dancing was in the twenties, thirties and forties when it could be claimed that everybody danced. Now, in the 1990s, ballroom dancing is no longer a national obsession. What happened to make this change, and does it spell the end of ballroom dancing?

Today 'ballroom dancing' of the old standard dances survives in a very few pockets in Scotland, notably in the Glasgow Plaza, the Star Ballroom in Dundee and the Aberdeen Beach Ballroom. Some hotels have dancing sessions and there are still dancing clubs and schools. Disco dancing is very much more popular but there is a division between those who disco and those who ballroom dance. An ability to ballroom dance does not presume an ability to disco and vice versa. The division is largely dictated by age. Discos are generally the province of the young. The story of dancing has often involved division. In the eighteenth and nineteenth centuries it was social class which decided who should dance. A burgeoning middle-class flocked to new ballrooms and barriers were removed. There was a period in late nineteenth and early twentieth centuries when dancing was open to all.

Another division occurred when, in the 1920s, the young became bored with the 'old' dances and war-time influences brought new exciting dances from America which had less appeal for older dancers.

At that time it seemed as if the young might take over and oust the adults from the dance floor but dancing teachers intervened, modifying the new steps and setting new standards. Self-preservation was probably as much a part of this as any desire to preserve the dances. To be able to teach a dance it is necessary to agree on the steps and to hold competitions it is necessary to establish standards.

This standardisation led to another split between 'social' dancers and 'competition' dancers. As competitions proliferated there was a tendency to formalise dress into the exaggerated styles displayed on the television programme, 'Come Dancing'. Although it was, and still is, hugely popular, some would argue that this programme created a false image of ballroom dancing. People began to think of ballroom dancing as an impossible dream involving technically difficult, cabaret-style displays of footwork and requiring expensive dresses and specially designed evening suits. Ballroom dancing appeared to be beyond the reach of the average man in the street and the idea of 'social dancing' as a regular weekly activity faded.

Another split occurred when the music changed during the forties and fifties. Musicians claim that when jazz and rock arrived, there were major changes in attitudes. People came to listen to the music and would crowd round the bandstands to listen instead of taking to the floor to dance.

It also happened that the new musicians were of a new school of thought. Following the anarchy of Skiffle and Rock, the newer bands could no longer read musical scores – a skill that would have involved study which was counter to the mood for improvisation and freedom of expression. Now they preferred to act instinctively and played 'by ear'. 'Anyone can play' meant that anyone did play, with unpredictable results.

In this climate the new music could have no strict tempo without which it became impossible to dance formal steps. Dancers were reduced to bobbing up and down in response to the music.

This was one factor which brought another change. Ballroom dancing was essentially an activity for two people who attempted to dance as one. The new style, which was to develop into disco dancing, was more the expression of an individual's response to the music. Partners were not required.

The emancipation of women and the late twentieth century emphasis on the importance of the individual have contributed to the change in popular dancing.

Once before, when the young developed their own dances and styles, the teachers were able to modify the dances and add them to the body of accepted styles which would suit most dancers in the ballrooms. This time round, circumstances were different. Standardising or watering-down disco would not bring back the crowds. Teachers did and still do teach disco, but their students are mainly the young. The frenzied activity and high noise level hold few attractions for the older generation whose tastes are different. The young are firmly established in the disco world and it may be that their reasons for dancing are different too.

In the past, ballroom dancing was a social activity which brought partners together in close physical contact. A boy could put his arms round a girl without formal introduction. It has been suggested that in a freer society there is no need to set up a contact which happens in any case.

Conversation during sets of Quadrilles or with a partner during a slow Waltz allowed dancers the opportunity to meet strangers in safe surroundings and assess whether they would like the contact to continue or not. It was a polite, social convenience to be able to refuse a dance and thereby discourage further friendship or to accept and develop a relationship. There were recognised conversational formulas which provided signals for partners. 'Do you come here often?' was the standard opener and the invitation to the last dance of the evening led to the inevitable 'Can I see you home?' This was the way many couples met and matched.

Now, at a time when freedom and emancipation have led to some confusion in the rôles of men and women, gestures suffice instead of words. The high level of noise which cuts off conversation may also cover the initial embarrassment of meeting new partners. Early elimination of unsuitable company can be achieved through dress. Designer labels meet matching or corresponding labels. Punk hair meets punk hair. Leathers meet leathers. Clothes and make-up are providing visual introductions.

While disco dancing is regarded as the preserve of the young, it also maintains a lower age limit because most discos are now licensed. This trend began in the early seventies when the big ballrooms in Glasgow were still packing in 2,000 dancers each night. At that time a licence for a building carried a legal age limit of 21. A licensed ballroom was therefore forced to exclude younger dancers. In Barrowland, for example, the introduction of the strict legal licensing limit entailed a drop in attendance from 2,000 to 300 or 400 a night within a few weeks. This had a disastrous effect on the ballroom dancing business. Not only were the under 21s obliged to find other entertainment, but they also missed out on the years of learning to dance by watching more experienced dancers. While social dancers did not always take formal lessons, they could and did develop skills painlessly by dancing three or four nights a week in the company of 'good' dancers. Nor was there much point in attending dance schools if the doors of the big ballrooms were to remain closed to the under 21s.

Today in Scotland, as indeed in the whole of Britain, ballroom dancing no longer holds a position of high prestige except in professional and amateur dance circles. This contrasts with many other countries, in Europe and beyond, where ballroom dancing is treated as a sport and is reported in the sports news. As a result it benefits from the kind of sponsorship and mass interest that attaches to sport.

This 'sporting' image has its appeal, but it is not without its dangers. The intense competition between top dancers, both professional and amateur, tends to develop an increase in showmanship. Television reports tend to show the 'best' dancers, thereby re-inforcing the mistaken idea that this is a pursuit for dedicated specialists only.

Other positive signs of continuing interest are the numbers of couples who book dancing lessons before they are married, so that they can dance the traditional first Waltz together. In the north of Scotland some couples prefer the Grand March, which is a walking dance reminiscent of the old Polonaise and serving the same purpose of allowing the ladies to display their dresses and at the same time involving the entire company in a social dance led off by the principal couple, the bride and groom.

There are still dinner-dances and dances on festive occasions like Christmas, when the ability to dance is regarded as a social asset. The traditional annual Highland Balls continue at the Skye Gathering, Blair Castle, Hopetoun House and several others.

The Assembly Rooms in Edinburgh hold fortnightly tea dances, and these are increasing in popularity in several centres across the country. Here, the emphasis tends to be on nostalgia, and there are few young dancers on the floor. The main difference is that where, formerly, tea dances were an opportunity to dance twice in one day, current tea dances tend to be held instead of evening dances. Aging dancers, including many women now widowed, prefer to stay at home on dark nights.

There are still pockets of young dancers who enjoy the challenge of the old style dances. At the time of writing there are strong ballroom dancing clubs at Edinburgh, Aberdeen and St Andrews Universities.

An Australian film, *Strictly Ballroom* was a major hit in 1991 and succeeded in transmitting some of the exhilaration and joy of dancing with a partner. Ballroom dance teachers were aware of an increased interest in classes following the release of the film. It remains to be seen whether the interest will grow or die away.

As with any leisure activity today, enthusiasts must face the hard facts of economics. The facts were reported in the Glasgow *Evening News* in 1927:

> The teaching of dancing and the provision of facilities for dancing have become a lively and profitable industry, giving occupation to far more men and women than are employed in all the theatres, music halls and picture houses put together . . . To keep the plant running in full operation as long as possible during a twenty-four hour day is a sound economic principle in the manufacturing world. It applies to the Dance trade also.

Seventy years later public tastes have changed. Music Halls have gone. Ballrooms have gone. In recent years there has been a renewal of public interest in theatres and cinemas but it seems unlikely that there will be a similar demand for ballrooms. Many of the buildings have been demolished and the silky floors have been smashed by the bulldozers. Some have been converted to Bingo halls, with fixing nails hammered into their sprung floors to anchor tables and chairs.

However, people have always danced and it is inconceivable that all forms of dancing will come to an end. Perhaps we are poised once again for a change of style. When it arrives we can be sure that the old will be shocked and the young will be excited, which is just as it should be.

Notes

CHAPTER 1

1   *Universal Etymological English Dictionary* (1740)
2   *Oxford English Dictionary* (2nd edition, 1989)
3   *Chambers Encyclopaedia* (1859–68)
4   *Oxford English Dictionary*
5   Edward Burt, *Letters from a Gentleman in the North of Scotland to His Friend in London* (1754)
6   John Knox to Mary Queen of Scots (1562)
7   *The Statistical Account of Scotland* (21 vols, 1791–1799)
8   Robert Chambers, *Traditions of Edinburgh* (1824), vol 1
9   John Jackson, *History of the Scottish Stage* (1793), p 418
10 Chambers, *Traditions of Edinburgh*, vol 1, pp 126, 134, 136, 199–202
11 Allan Ramsay, *The Fair Assembly* (1723)
12 Robert Chambers, *Domestic Annals of Scotland from the Revolution to the Rebellion of 1745* (1861), vol 3
13 Captain E Dunbar, *Social Life in Former Days* (1865)
14 Burt, *Letters From a Gentleman*
15 Chambers, *Domestic Annals*, vol 3, pp 590–91
16 Burt, *Letters From a Gentleman*
17 *Scots Peerage*, vol 7, p 26
18 Alexander Carlyle, *Autobiography* (1860), p 74
19 Nestor, *Rambling Recollections of Old Glasgow* (1880)
20 Senex (Robert Reid), *Glasgow Past and Present* (1856), vol 2, p 111
21 *The Old Glasgow Club* (1908–1912), vol 2
22 Mackintosh, *History of Civilisation in Scotland* (1892–6), p 419
23 Sir Alexander Boswell, *Edinburgh or the Ancient Royalty: a Sketch of Former Manners (1810)*
24 A Fergusson, *The Honourable Henry Erskine* (1882), pp 109–117
25 Chambers, *Traditions of Edinburgh*, vol 2, p 27
26 Chambers,*Traditions of Edinburgh*, vol 1, p 27
27 Boswell, *Edinburgh or the Ancient Royalty*
28 Chambers, *Traditions of Edinburgh*, vol 2, pp 108–112
29 Edward Topham, *Letters From Edinburgh in the Years 1774 and 1745* (1780), vol 2, pp 156 and 574
30 Oliver Goldsmith's *Collected Letters* (ed K C Balderston 1928), p 11
31 Minutes of Edinburgh Assembly
32 D M Malloch, *The Book of Glasgow Anecdote* (1912)
33 Topham, *Letters From Edinburgh*

34 *Book of the Old Edinburgh Club*, vol 19, p 62
35 Topham, *Letters from Edinburgh*, p 262
36 *Book of the Old Edinburgh Club*, vol 19
37 Lord Cockburn, *Memorials of His Time* (1856)
38 *Edinburgh Courant*, 22 February 1775; 11 March 1775
39 Hugo Arnot, *History of Edinburgh* (1779), vol 3, p 383
40 *Edinburgh Courant*, 5 January 1758
41 Arnot, *History of Edinburgh*, vol 3, p 383
42 *Book of Old Edinburgh Club*, vol 19
43 *Book of Old Edinburgh Club*, vol 19
44 Minutes of Edinburgh Assembly
45 James Denholm, *The History of Glasgow* (1804)
46 A H Franks, *Social Dance* (1963)

CHAPTER 2

1 *Glasgow Courier*, 9 April 1812
2 Franks, *Social Dance*, p 130
3 Cecil Sharp and A P Oppe, *The Dance* (1924)
4 *Times*, 12 July 1816 and 16 July 1816
5 Lord Byron, 'The Waltz – An Apostrophic Hymn'
6 Lord Byron, *English Bards and Scotch Reviewers* (1809)
7 Belinda Quirey, *May I have The Pleasure?* (1976)
8 Barclay Dun, *Quadrilles* (1818)
9 *Spectator* (1711)
10 *Times*, March 1844
11 J P Flett and T M Flett, *Traditional Dancing in Scotland* (1964)
12 David Anderson, *Ballroom Guide* (1888)
13 Henry Grey Graham, *Social Life in Scotland in the Eighteenth Century* (various editions)
14 D C Cuthbertson, *Quaint Scots of Bygone Days* (1939), p 116
15 Eleanor Sillar, *Edinburgh's Child* (1961)
16 Max O'Rell, *Friend MacDonald* (1887)
17 Franks, *Social Dance*, p 125
18 P J S Richardson, *Social Dances of the Nineteenth Century in England* (1960), p 120

CHAPTER 3

1 Edinburgh *Evening News*, February 1900
2 Anderson, *Ballroom Guide*
3 Dundee *Courier*, 18 November 1989
4 Flett and Flett, *Traditional Dancing in Scotland*
5 Dundee *Courier*
6 Franks, *Social Dance*

CHAPTER 4

1   Franks, *Social Dance*, p 166
2   Frances Rust, *Dance in Society* (1969), p 83
3   Sharp and Oppe, *The Dance*
4   Edinburgh *Evening News*, 1 January 1920
5   Edinburgh *Evening News*, 1 January 1920
6   Edinburgh *Evening News*, 1 December 1920
7   Edinburgh *Evening News*, 4 December 1920

CHAPTER 5

1   Rust, *Dance in Society*, p 89
2   Victor Sylvester, *Dancing is My Life* (1958), p 88
3   Curt Sachs, *World History of the Dance* (1933), p 445
4   *Edinburgh Evening Dispatch*, 1922
5   Lew Grade, *Still Dancing – My Story* (1987)
6   Edinburgh *Evening News*, October 1921
7   *Dundee Telegraph*, December 1929

CHAPTER 6

1   Quirey, *May I Have the Pleasure?*, p 88
2   Rust, *Dance in Society*, p 99
3   Franks, *Social Dance*, p 189
4   Sylvester, *Dancing is My Life*

CHAPTER 7

1   *Melody Maker*, February 1949

CHAPTER 8

1   Victor Sylvester, *Modern Ballroom Dancing* (1974)
2   Franks, *Social Dance*
3   Imperial Society of Teachers of Dancing, *Teach Yourself Ballroom Dancing* (1977)
4   Sid Colin, *And the Bands Played On* (1977)
5   Rust, *Dance in Society*
6   Quirey, *May I Have the Pleasure?*
7   Rust, *Dance in Society*
8   Rust, *Dance in Society*
9   Edinburgh *Evening News*
10 Edinburgh *Evening News*, 1 March 1975

11 Sylvester, *Modern Ballroom Dancing*
12 I S T D, *Teach Yourself Ballroom Dancing*
13 Colin, *And the Bands Played On*
14 Edinburgh *Evening News*, September 1979

Appendix 1

BALLROOMS	Opened	Closed
The Albert	1905 (30 May)	1965
Albert Palais de Danse	1925	
Alhambra	1894 (4 December)	
Aberdeen Beach Ballroom	1929 (3 May)	
Barrowland	1934 (December)	1958
(re-opened)	1960	1974
Blackpool Tower	1894 (August)	
Blackpool Palace	1904 (July)	
Burmah, Kirkcaldy	ca.1935	
Cadora Rest, Glasgow	1932	
Caledonian Hotel, Inverness	1939	
Cavendish	1939	1939
Chalet, Broughty Ferry	1933	
Del Mar	1937 (September)	
Dennistoun Palais	1922	1936
(re-opened)	1938	1962
Dundee Palais	1977	
Dunedin, Edinburgh	ca.1922	
Eldorado, Edinburgh	1931 (23 December)	
Empress, Dundee	1938	
Excelsior	1933	1948
(re-opened)	1956	
F & F Palais	1948	
Fountainbridge Palais	1920 (24 December)	1967/68
Grafton Assembly Rooms (re-opened as Maxime's)	1920 (December)	
Green's Playhouse	1927	1987 (demolished)
Happy Valley	1933 (September)	
Hibs Ballroom	1934	
Imperial Palais, Glasgow		
Locarno, Glasgow	1926 (December)	1929
(re-opened)	1934 (19 December)	1936
Locarno, Edinburgh	1936 (30 October)	
Majestic, Glasgow	1972	
Marine Gardens	1909 (31 May)	1939
Maxime's	1921 (October)	1938 (12 April)
New Dunedin	1937	
New Cavendish	1940	1962
(from 1972 open as Clouds/Coasters/Bermuda Triangle/Hoochie Coochie Club/Outer Limits)		
New Troxy (Kirkcaldy)	1935	

Norwood House, Glasgow	1921 (November)	1935
Picadilly Club, Glasgow	1926	1936
Plaza, Glasgow	1922 (27 December)	to date
Plaza, Edinburgh	1926 (September)	1975 (1 March)
Red Barn/Cameo, Glasgow	1939 (30 March)	
Rothesay Pavilion	1938	
Silver Slipper	1938 (September)	
West End Ballroom	1934	
Westfield Hall	1932	
Winter Gardens, Empress	1897	

Appendix 2

SOME OF THE MANY BALLROOMS DESTROYED BY FIRE

The Albert (1974)
Assembly Rooms (High Street), Edinburgh (1824)
Bermuda Triangle (1985)
Barrowland (1958)
Blackpool Tower (1956, re-opened 1958)
Dundee Palais (1977)
Dunedin Palais (1932)
Dennistoun Palais (1936)
Eldorado (1984)
F & F Palais (1948)
Maxime's (1932, re-opened 1933)
New Berkeley (1939)
New Troxy (1935, re-built as the Burmah)
Picadilly Club, Glasgow (1936)

Index

Adam, James 7
Adamson, Alexander 35
Albert Ballroom 27,30, 41, 46, 47, 49–50,
    56, 59, 62, 65, 68, 69, 80, 86, 89, 91, 93,
    99, 100, 103, 104, 114, 117–118
Albert, Prince (husband of Queen
    Victoria) 30
Alhambra Ballroom 28
Allemande 12, 18, 19
Almack's 19
Ambrose 65
American Barn Dance 24
Anderson, David 25
Argyll, George Duke of 7
Arnot, Mr 15
assemblies 1, 3–5, 7, 9–10, 12–14, 18, 31
Assembly Close 4
assembly rooms 2, 7, 9, 10, 13, 15–17, 25,
    26, 31, 47, 55, 61, 106, 126, 129
Ayr Ballroom 54

Babbity Bowster 22
badges 9
Bailie Fife's Close 9
Ball (defined) 1
Bantam championships 87
Barn Dance 12, 24, 40
Barrowland 76, 81, 89, 94, 97, 98, 101,
    102, 104, 106, 114, 116, 118, 121, 129
Bathgate, Andrew 74
Bayle, Mr 14
Bee-Baw-Babbity 22
Belsches, Williamina 14
Bell's Wynd 5
Berkeley Ballroom 54, 62, 74, 77
Birling 78
Black Bottom 52
Blair Castle 27
Blue Beat 117

Blue Danube 21
Blue Mariners 95
Blue Rockets 95, 104
Bogle, Nancy 7
bongraces 3
Bonnard, Francis 13, 14
Bonnet, Madame 12
Boomps-a-Daisy 70
Boston (dance) 38–9, 41, 43, 44, 47, 108
Boswell, Sir Alexander 9
Brahms, Johannes 21
Bremner, Robert 8
'Brose and Butter' 8
Brown, Mr and Mrs Warren, snr 122
Brown, Warren, jnr 123
Bunny Hug 41
Burns, Donny 123, 124
Burt, Edward 6
Byron, Lord 19

Cakewalk 29
calashes 3
Caledonian Hall 25
Caledonian Hunt 16, 25
capuchins 3
Carioca 68
Carlyle, Dr Alexander 7
Casani, Santos 49, 60
Cavendish Ballroom 47, 86
Chambers, Robert 3
Chapman, Jack 80
Charleston 50–2, 59, 62, 68, 70, 120, 126
Chestnut Tree 92
Chisholm, George 95, 118
Chopin, Frédéric 21
Cinderella Waltz 75
Circassian Circle 22
Circle dances 24
Cockburn, Lord 13

Comely Gardens 14
Contredance 12, 18, 22, 27
Corri, Signor 15
Cotillon 8, 12, 19, 22, 40
Country Dance 7, 8, 10–12, 16, 18, 24–5, 31, 67
Creech (publisher) 12

'D'ye ken John Peel' 26
Dance floors 19, 55–6
Dancing Times 28
Dashing White Sergeant 22
Dawn, Dorothy 50, 69, 88
Delfont, Bert and Al 59
Dennistoun Palais 53, 54, 62, 68, 74, 81, 89
Diamond's Academy 53, 100
Diamond, Joe 31
Digges, Mr 14
directress 6, 8–13, 17
Disco 119–21, 126–29
Don, Lady 14
Dow, Daniel 8
Drummelier, Lady 6
Dundas, George and Bertha 64
Dundee Palais 64, 75, 92, 93, 96, 98
Dunedin Palais 33
Dunn, Barclay 22
Dunvegan Castle 27

Ecossaise 18
Edinburgh Courant 14
Edward VII 31
Eightsome Reel 26, 67, 87, 113
Elimination Dance 72
Empire line 28
Empress Ballroom 28
English Country Dance 13
Excelsior Ballroom 91
Excuse-me Dance 71

Fair Assembly 4
Fairweather, Gaynor 123, 124
fans 4, 8
Fergusson, A 9
'Flowers of Edinburgh' 8, 24
Formation dancing 22, 52, 88–9, 111, 112
Fountainbridge Palais 47

Fox Trot 31, 47, 52, 71, 85, 108
Freeman, Louis 44, 45, 72, 73
Freer, Alex 80

Galliard 12
Galop 23, 31, 67
garters 3
Gaybirds 76, 97, 98, 104, 116
George IV 25
George Square, Edinburgh 13, 25
George Street, Edinburgh 15
Glencairn, Countess 9
Glendinning's Dancing School 32, 33
Goldsmith, Oliver 10
Gow, Nathaniel 27
Gow, Neil 27
Graham, Captain 16
Grand March 37
Green's Playhouse 54, 62, 64, 68, 74, 82, 89–90, 112
Grizzly Bear 41

Hall, Henry 81, 101
Hamilton, William 3, 9
Hanley, Cliff 102
Hanley, Danny 33
Happy Valley 68, 80, 86
Hesitation Waltz 43
Highland ball 27
Highland Reel 12
Highland Schottische 24
Hokey Cokey 71
Holyrood 5, 15
hooped dresses 3, 28
Hopetoun, Countess 9
Hopetoun House 27
Horn Order 2
Hunter's Academy 33

Imperial Ballroom 62, 74, 80, 87
Imperial College 33
Imperial Society of Dance Teachers 38, 44, 52, 120
Irish Jig 24
Irvine, Bill and Bobby 123, 124

Jazz 43–7, 68, 106, 110, 118, 128
Jigs 12

Jitterbug 68, 93, 94, 102, 105, 126
Jive 94, 105, 122
Jones, Bobby 54
Judy Walk 41

Kennedy, Mrs 17
Kennedy, Susanna, Duchess of Eglinton 4
Kirkbraehead 15
Kirkcudbright, Lord 10
Knees-Up-Mother-Brown 70
Knox, John 1
Kosmo Club 83–4

Lambeth Walk 70
Lancers 22, 26, 30–2, 40, 50, 67, 108
Lanner, Joseph 21
lappet 3
Latin American dance 109–10, 118
Lehar, Franz 21
Lennard, Jose 47, 60
Leven, Countess of 9
Linton, Ena 33
Locarno Ballroom 53, 60, 62, 74, 86,
    88–90, 92, 94, 97, 99–102, 121
Loss, Joe 54, 75, 97
Lothian, Andy 75, 92, 93, 96, 99

McCall, Tommy 82
Macdonald's School of Dancing 32
MacEwan, James B 31
MacGregor, Billy 76, 89, 97–9, 106, 114,
    116, 121
MacLennan, D G 31
MacNaughton, J D 31
MacQueen, Mr 12
MacRae, Farquhar 53, 62, 111
Madison 118–9
Mansfield, Earl of 12
Marathon dancing 66
Marine Gardens 36–7, 40, 43, 56–60, 65,
    66, 70, 81–2, 86–9, 91, 93, 97, 103
Martell, Lena 114
Martin, Mr 12
Mary, Queen of Scots 1
Masked Ball 14
Masquerade 1, 3, 25
Maxime's 61, 84, 85
Maxixe 43, 109

Mazourka 33
Merrilees, William 83–5
Miller, Glen 96
Mills, Annette 51, 70
Mintoun, Lady 9
Minto, Lady 9
Minuet 3, 9–13, 16–18, 21, 27
'Moll Pately' 22
'Monymusk' 8
Moonlight Waltz 32
Moray, Earl of 15
Morton, Tam 54, 55
Murray of Claremont, Lady 9
Murray, Nicky 9, 10

Nash, Beau 2
negligees 3
Neill, James 35
Newhall, Lady 6
North Berwick, Lady 6
Norwood Ballroom 49, 62, 77

Ogg, Peter 47, 64, 84
Old Time 31, 37–8, 87, 105, 108, 113
One-Step 41, 43, 44, 47
O'Rell, Max 27
Ormiston, Lady 6

Palais Glide 71
Palais de Plaisir 65
Panmure, Countess of 6
Patrick Steil's Close 4
Paul Jones 71
Peacock, Francis 8
Peers, Donald 82
penny weddings 2
Petronella 24
petticoats 3
plaids 3
Plaza Ballroom, Edinburgh 61, 62, 77–9,
    90, 119
Plaza Ballroom, Glasgow 54, 68, 74, 80,
    81, 82, 89, 93, 99, 101, 111, 121, 127
Polka 23, 24, 26, 36, 40, 43, 70
Polonaise 23, 28
Poorhouse of Edinburgh 6
Proscription of Highland dress 8, 27

Quadrille 22, 25, 26, 31, 33, 47, 50, 67, 128
Queen Charlotte 17, 19, 25
Queen Victoria 21, 24, 30
Quickstep 52, 62, 71, 77, 85, 100, 108, 117

Raeburn, Elizabeth 57
Ragtime, 29, 43, 44
Ramsay, Allan 3, 4
Ranelach Garden 15
Reel 8, 12, 13, 22, 24, 26, 27, 31, 33, 47
Register dancing 101
Reid, John 35
Riddell, John 8
Ridotto 1, 14
Rochhead, Mrs 14
Rock and Roll 115, 116, 122, 126
Rory o' More 24
Roscoe, Adela 50
Rout 1
Royal Infirmary 6
Rumba 68, 77, 101, 109, 110, 122

Samba 44, 109, 122
Schottische 24, 27, 67
Scotch Reel 24
Scott, Sir Walter 14, 25
Scottish Country Dancing 22
sedan chairs 15, 17
Selkirk, Earl of 2
Senex 7
Sequence Dancing 31
Shake 46, 49, 71, 116
Sharp, Adam 111, 121
Shawfield, Mrs Campbell of 9
Shimmy 45, 46
Sielle, Robert 51
Sillar, Eleanor 26
Ska 117
Skinner, James Scott 8
Skye Gathering 27
Skyrockets 95, 104
Spectator 22
Spot Dance 72
Smead, Harry 75
Squadronaires 95, 103–4
Square Dance 24
Star Ballroom 119, 120

State Balls 31
stays 3
Stevenlaw's Close 5
Stewart's Academy 46
Stirling, James 9
stomachers 3
Strange, Mr 12
Strathspey 8, 12, 13, 26
Strauss, Johann 21
Strip the Willow 22, 24
St Andrew's Halls 54, 62, 77, 104
Stuart, Anne 4
Stungo, Symon 80
Subscription dances 18, 31
Swing 21, 68, 70, 71, 84, 91, 95, 101, 110
Sylvester, Victor 41, 52, 60, 94, 108

Tango 41, 43, 47, 49, 50, 52, 57, 59, 62, 67, 76, 77, 84, 85, 92, 108, 111, 119
Tea Dances 24, 45, 93
'Television Dancing Club' 106
Theatre Royal, Edinburgh 14
tobacco lords 7
Tontine Society 7
Topham, Edward 10, 12, 13
Tower Ballroom 28
Traquair House 27
Turkey Trot 41
Twist 116, 120, 126

Union Ball 25

Valentine, Bert 66, 67, 95, 105
Vauxhall Gardens 14, 15
Veleta 24, 38, 50, 108
Viennese Waltz 21
Volta 19
voucher system 18

Waldorf Ballroom 54, 62
Waltz 19, 21–4, 26, 32, 37–41, 43, 47, 49, 50, 52, 53, 57, 62, 67, 70, 71, 76, 77, 84, 85, 96, 101, 103, 108, 119, 128, 129
Waltz Country Dance 22
Warren, Alex 31, 32, 41, 45, 47, 49, 50, 86, 88, 89, 91, 93, 94, 97, 103, 104, 114, 118
Warren, Anne 31, 32, 41, 50, 88

Warren, Annie 31, 32, 41, 49, 50
Warren, Jessie 31, 32, 41, 49, 50
Warren, John, snr. 31, 32, 41, 50, 117
Warren, John 31, 32, 41, 50, 68, 69, 100, 118
Warren, Valerie 117
Washington Post 29

Watson, James 25
Weber, Karl Maria Von 21
West Bow, Edinburgh 2, 3
Woman's Life 21, 30
Wood, Chalmers 74
Wood, Charlie 37, 38
Wright, Tim 61, 114